A Boy, His Surfboard and the Storm

A true story

Cheri Kane

Kimberly!
no matter the storm, He is
over all!
Cheri Kane

MERRY ROBIN PUBLISHING

Merry Robin Publishing

Book Cover by Merry Robin Publishing

1st edition 2023

Library of Congress Control Number: 2023906591

Published in partnership with Merry Robin Publishing, LLC

To explore more of our published titles, please visit www.Life-OnPurpose.com/books

In loving memory of my mother, Joy Ashton-Downs,
for teaching me how to pray at a very early age.

To my daughters, Melissa and Becky,
who never gave up praying that night.

To Jaren, my Buck-A-Roo,
who endured the tempest of that long, cold night and never gave up.

Contents

Prologue

It is Monday, January 9, 2023 and California is facing one of the most damaging rain events in decades. Many have lost their homes and even their lives due to the extreme flooding and destruction. Crops are destroyed and roads washed out. All is in turmoil for so many who are facing the uncertainty of what their future might hold. Hearts are failing, and lives altered. Faith is faltering and hope is fading quickly for so many of these victims.

As is witnessed by news stations all around, the reality and aftermath of these storm events can never be fully realized unless witnessed first-hand. The tremendous force of such storm events is always accompanied with high surf, fierce winds, damaging mudslides and flooding, destroying homes, crops and people's livelihoods, and worse: taking the lives of many, young *and* old. Even the mountains of California are seeing unprecedented snow fall, adding to the commotion and apprehension for so many.

California storm events such as these always bring back vivid memories of the night we lost our sixteen-year-old son, Jaren, at sea. It was a harrowing night and to this day, I shudder when the hours of that night play before me like a carefully preserved movie, archived in the back of my mind.

During that night, I would face many truths about myself, about God and about His purposes. I would learn that everyone has a purpose in this life. Some would live to fulfill theirs here on earth, while others would be called back home at a time many of us might think was too soon and too unfulfilled. I have come to understand that God truly is over all and that if lives seem to be unfairly cut short, there is an eternal plan and this life as we know it is just a speck of time in God's divine design. I have come to better understand and find peace in the fact that although some such lives seem to be cut short, God will not allow their purposes to go unfinished and somehow the purposes of each are being continually fulfilled beyond this mortal life.

On the night Jaren was ripped out to sea in a violent storm, there would be three lives lost. A young mother and her infant baby girl, killed in a car accident and a man who was working on shore. All so terrible and unfair with the incomprehensible grief their loved ones would be faced with. Each life lost that night would make one think; "Where is God?"

I hope those of you who read this story, or who have lost loved ones so unfairly, will be able to recognize the tender mercies and love of an Omnipresent God who's plan we cannot always understand. That's okay. We are all on this path to learn of Him and of our place in His Grand Eternal Design. I hope you come away with a greater sense of His love and concern for you and the personal path you are on. I hope you come away with greater faith and hope that one day, all will be well and all tears will be wiped away. I also hope you come away with a greater desire to live up to your full potential each day, because none of us know when we will be called back home to that very God who gave us life.

Chapter One

Have You Ever Experienced the Majesty?

Have you ever experienced the majesty of the mighty Pacific Ocean as she hurls her waves onto shore? Have you stood along the shoreline waiting for the next set of waves in anticipation only to be more amazed at the strength in which they come rumbling in? Have you felt the exhilarating rush of the cold splash and listened in awe to the thunderous noise as they come charging in? It's as if a thousand hands are joyously applauding while each new wave takes its final bow.

Unconsciously, I am serenaded with the chattering sounds of the overhead flock of seagulls intertwined with the near and far voices of beach goers. All senses become so enlivened in those mystical moments of the ocean with its unmistakable aroma, making each beach-going experience all the more magical.

I love standing ankle deep and feeling the tug and grasp as the water rushes in, then back out again. I love to feel the tickle of tiny sea shells, seaweed, and rocks dancing around my feet, mingling with my toes. To me, the ocean is a woman with a vibrant array of personalities. I have witnessed her many moods at different times of the day and night and season. I have witnessed as the ocean eerily takes on a manic persona as storms begin to brew overhead. At will, she is able to morph into any mood that can't be hindered by the force of man or of nature. The ocean always seems to be in charge. Even in her mighty chaos, she strikes the rules and sets new boundaries of her own making.

How humbling it is to know that the ocean truly exhibits a life and power all her own. At one moment she will seem gentle, serene and calm. Yet within a very short span of time, she can clamor into a tumultuous churning of frothy waves, heaving herself into vigorous disruption.

Like a chameleon, the ocean always mirrors the energy of the atmosphere. On a clear sunny day, the ocean is a beautiful reflection of blue and green hues dotted with glistening white capped waves. On a cold cloudy day, the ocean's color is a melancholy gray, reflecting the thick blanket fog while somber waves meander to shore.

I have waded and played in waves that seem to tumble onto shore with no particular hurry or rhythm. The ocean is unperturbed by the bustling world around her. She moves about to her own rhythm and mood. Some days, the ocean's waves come blasting in with such force as if to warn me not to stray too far into the water.

"Red tide" is another of the ocean's personality displays and happens seldomly. It is caused when a type of algae blooms so numerous that it causes vibrant, coastal discoloration upon the surface of the ocean, creating a fluorescent glow at night. How can I attempt to describe such a rare occasion which can be witnessed only at night? I have only been able to witness this phenomena a handful of times. To fully appreciate this, you must see it at night when the sky is clear and the moon full. During these nights, it would seem as though the moon, the ocean's nighttime companion, has taken on a whole new role in the sky, giving each spectator a more brilliant experience below as now, he appears as a bright spotlight, positioned perfectly above to illuminate the surface of the ocean. To see the fluorescent blues, purples, oranges and reds is a sight indeed! They shimmer like the fresh whimsical brushstrokes of an oil painting. The free flowing wisps of colors dance and mingle together on the surface as the waves gently roll beneath.

When seeing it for myself, I wondered if the fish below were also captivated by this extraordinary display overhead. Could they know they also played a very important role in the red tide? Their movement along with the currents of the ocean are the brushstrokes that create the flow of the swirling flourescent colors of the algae bloom. They always leave a trail of fluorescent colors as they swim about. Unfortunately for the fish, the red tide is the product of too much algae, which can be toxic and harmful to both fish and humans. Even so, the ocean has a way of being beautiful even when she is most dangerous.

When I think of the ocean, of her danger, power, and beauty, her waves come automatically to mind. Waves are monitored by the wind. Because of this, the wind plays a big part in how the waves will be at any given time. If it is blowing from offshore, the waves are usually flattened out or very small. Yet when the wind is blowing out to sea, the waves stack up nicely. These are the types of waves surfers, wind surfers, body surfers and boogie boarders live for!

On the very rare occasions of major storms in Southern California, the ocean becomes muddy brown, with enormous waves tossing all kinds of debris that has been helplessly washed out from nearby river bottoms and coastal campgrounds. It is unwise to be too close to the ocean during these storms when she is manifesting her most destructive powers. I can attest to this. I have watched from a distance with a sense of wonder and sadness as beachfront properties toppled like toys from what had once been their securely concreted, shoreline perches. Sadly, they fell victims of the storm-tossed sea, along with toppled trees, breaking like splintered toothpicks. Nothing can withstand the ocean's power when she decides to exhibit her strength.

During one of these storms, I saw a crumpled camper shell and other unrecognizable objects bobbing about as the mountainous waves increased in size and strength, taking on the appearance and sound of thunderous concrete clashing against everything in their path.

Many times I have stood on the historic Ventura Pier in delight and watched as waves burst over its deck and up through the planks at the outer end of the pier. Each time I felt an exhilarating rush as the longest and oldest wooden pier on the whole Pacific West Coast, would rock back and forth like a cradle.

As with other spectators, I stood there in childlike anticipation, waiting for the next set of waves beneath to come exploding up through the planks beneath. The force of these waves would rival Yellowstone's famous Old Faithful Geyser! An incredible sight to see!

People would gather along the shoreline and on the pier, all enjoying the grand spectacle of the ocean. Before long, the pier was closed off by the lifeguards shouting warnings to everyone: "Too Dangerous!" "Stay Off!" while locking the wide gate of the pier entrance. This gate is only ever closed in serious times of storm.

From this point, I, like many others, would move to higher ground and continue to enjoy the fascinating show as the mighty Pacific Ocean put on yet another spectacle of her magnificent performances. No spectator goes away disappointed at the strength and velocity with which she relentlessly slams herself towards shore during such storm events as these.

At these times, I never gave any thought as to just how dangerous this could be. Yet, at the same time I also instinctively knew not to go all the way out to the end of the pier when the waves got that big. I would even bring my three young children to watch while making sure to keep a good amount of distance between us and the waves. We had so much fun as we shared in the excitement of these moments during Californian storms. I was to learn later just how little I understood about the seriousness or power of the ocean. The threat of her power would shape my life in a way that I never anticipated when I sat watching the storm-tossed sea with my children in tow. Never in my wildest imagination would I think this magnificent Pacific Ocean might one day become my worst nightmare and unmerciful enemy.

I had always loved the many faces of the ocean's majestic nature. Now, as I remember back on my memories of her, I am struck by how there would come a day that I would be painfully made aware of her indiscriminating ability to take, destroy, or change a life that crossed her destructive path.

Chapter Two

Surfing, One of His Passions

M eet my son, Jaren. I call him "Buck-A-Roo!" At sixteen years old, he had already mastered the skateboard and won many awards with his skill as a champion skateboarder for his age bracket in the Southern California region. With knots in my stomach, I would watch as he performed his maneuvers on the halfpipe while effortlessly flipping above it through the air. To this day, I cringe when I remember the stunts he could pull off. By this time, he had also taken an interest in the guitar and was becoming quite musically inclined. It seemed like he could accomplish anything he set his mind to do.

About two weeks before his sixteenth birthday, I went looking to purchase a wetsuit for him at a local surf shop. Because I knew so little about surfing, I was surprised at how expensive wetsuits were. At the time, my budget was rather limited and wouldn't allow me to buy one of the nice new ones, and so I went looking for any used suits they might have.

I was relieved and a bit embarrassed to find that they had used wetsuits to sell at all.

While looking at my options, I had an impression that my son should have a thicker suit, even though it would cut even further into my limited budget. Worried about the cost, I quickly brushed the thought away and continued to search through the other less expensive options. However, even as I looked through suits I could better afford, I couldn't ignore the impression that Jaren needed a thicker wetsuit. Finally, I decided to trust my intuition. I gave in and picked out the thicker, and to my own anxiety, most expensive one on the rack.

Soon, I found myself standing there at the checkout line making a much more expensive purchase than I had anticipated and wondering how I was going to make my money stretch throughout the next couple of weeks. But I pushed these thoughts to the back of my mind because I was excited about being able to give Jaren a wetsuit for his birthday!

Chapter Three

Happy Birthday, Buck-A-Roo!

Two weeks later, on September 11, 1995, Jaren hit the big sixteen! Arising before sunup, I already knew that this was going to be a great day! His eyes lit up when he found the awkwardly wrapped gift was a wetsuit. Soon we were both dressed and out the door with his surfboard poking out from the sunroof of my car and his new (used) wetsuit in tow. We drove to "C" Street, Ventura's favorite surf spot, only minutes away from my apartment.

Perfectly stacked waves could be seen as we pulled into the parking lot. The sun was barely coming up behind on the eastern horizon and already, eager surfers were paddling out to catch the waves. The clamoring of seagulls added to the excitement as they hastily searched for their next meal on shore and in trash bins along the promenade.

The mists and aroma of the ocean beckoned Jaren into her tumbling waves. I believe I was the happiest of anyone on the shore that morning as

I watched my son paddle out and catch his first wave. He seemed to glide effortlessly back to shore with each wave he caught. I wanted to shout out to everyone nearby: "HEY! THAT'S MY SON!" But that would only embarrass him. So, with the widest of grins and proudest of feelings, I just watched, feeling as though I could burst at the seams. Barely able to contain myself, I managed to keep my exuberance and joy within as I gleefully cheered him on while watching from a distance.

It feels as if that day were only yesterday. Oh, how I enjoyed watching him from shore that morning as he was instinctively able to catch and ride each wave back to shore. He has always been a natural at just about everything he has put his mind to do, and this was no exception.

After about an hour of surfing, followed by a quick pancake, eggs and bacon breakfast at the nearby Denny's Restaurant, I hurried him off to school moments before the morning bell rang. It truly was a very good day, and I drove away exuberant!

Chapter Four

Who Says It Never Rains in Southern California?

Two months later, on Tuesday December 13, 1995, the most anticipated rainstorm in a long while was finally making its way to the Southern California coast with the projection of much needed moisture for our drought-stricken areas and crops. This wasn't to be just any old rainstorm. This was forecasted to be much more powerful than usual with the likelihood of dangerously high surf, flash flooding, and wind damage. Radio and TV news warnings were issued and continued to be updated throughout the day with mounting anticipation.

I had called to check in with my kids after school. My daughter Becky answered the phone. I let her know of my dinner meeting that evening at Spanish Hills Country Club. We chatted a bit about her day at school, and the rain, then cheerfully said our goodbyes. Becky would later recall that Jaren and three of his buddies, Jesse, Mark, and Chris, had headed to the beach to go surfing shortly after my call.

I can only imagine for a teenage surfer like my son, this day was promising to be the day of the "perfect storm." I'm sure for him, Jesse, Chris, and Mark, school was a burden and couldn't let out soon enough. It had been raining off and on since morning, and they knew the waves would be larger than usual. They were anxious to conquer the stormy surf.

When the school bell finally rang, with excitement and a jolt of adrenaline, the boys raced out of the school. They were finally free and were off to the beach with surfboards, boogie boards and wetsuits, ready for the conquest. By this time, the rain was building in intensity, and gusts of wind hollered, as if a decree of Mother Nature's grand fury was finally here at last! Now more than ever, enlivened by the energy of the atmosphere playing out around them, these young friends were off to capture the adventures that lay ahead! They were unaware of just how threatening Mother Nature would prove herself to be that day.

By now, the afternoon news broadcasters had sounded the alert for traffic snarls, high winds and surf, and flooding in some of the low lying areas.

While the storm was gaining power, these boys were heading up Highway 101 towards the Faria Beach Gated Community at Pitas Point, a few miles north of Ventura.

Were they taking bets with each other as to who would be able to catch the first wave? Who would ride the longest wave back to shore? Surely, they must have taunted each other as to who might be "the chicken" if the waves were too big.

But young and fearless were these friends! So off to high adventures they headed, without any thought of the impending danger that might be awaiting them on the shoreline.

As they neared their destination, the ocean was now in full sight. They must have felt a huge lump in their throats as they saw the scene playing out before them in the distance. It was apparent that the rain and wind-pelted waves crashed erratically onto shore as if ignoring all laws of nature and boundaries of the shoreline.

Would excitement now turn towards trepidation as the coastal highway brought them closer to their favorite surf destination? What would be going through their minds as they reached the nearest parking spot? Surfers who had usually dotted the waves were nowhere in sight, and the ocean was much more turbulent than anticipated.

Regardless of the moment, which of these four friends would now give into the slightest hint of fear? Who would be "the chicken"?

Despite any trepidation they may have felt, each leaped out of the car. Within a few feet, they were slipping through the private gate of Faria Beach, as they had done so many times before.

Of all the beach locations, public or private, this was by far one of their favorite locations for surfing. The angle of the shoreline seemed more accommodating for the size and length of the waves, giving any surfer a more exhilarating ride on perfectly arched waves as they barreled in towards the shore.

They were now experts at scaling the concrete wall of this gated community that separated the beachfront homes from the shoreline. First flinging their surfboards, boogie boards and wetsuits over to the other side, they hoisted themselves over.

I wonder if they felt a sense of awe while each was tugging at the zipper and leash of his wetsuit. But then again, they were sixteen-year-old boys, who were distracted by the excitement they felt to jump into the water.

Who would be the first to "chicken out"? "Not me," each might have thought to himself, as his apprehension was already beginning to mount within him. Who would be the first to let on to the others that this time he wasn't taking any chances, recognizing that his adrenaline rush was swirling with fear at what could happen? Would each of them recognize the warning signs of the veracity of the waves, as if in their angry fury they were shouting out to them, "Enter At Your Own Risk!"

Here they were: four invincible teenage boys who had been visualizing this moment all day long! Certainly, they might have been fantasizing about the stories they would tell their friends at school the next day, detailing how gnarly the waves were and how they conquered and divided each wave they pierced through with their boards. Is there any doubt that each would unflinchingly outline every detail with expanding exaggerations of every wave they conquered? Now it was evident that there would be no need for any exaggeration about this!

Leaping through wet sand with cautious excitement on each face, they scrambled even closer to the water's edge. As they came to the reality of their situation when looking at their now flimsy-seeming boards against the power of the ocean, their jaws must have dropped and their eyes widened. There was no question in any of their minds now that this could prove to be a disastrous attempt. They would quickly understand that the chaotic waves weren't a welcome invitation today.

Logical hesitation must have been the drum beat of their pounding hearts. They were now standing where the water meets the shore. The deafening sounds of the hollering wind and pelting rain were other warning signs not to be ignored.

At this point, the ocean showed no signs of mercy for anyone who dared enter her tirade. Majestic fury was now playing out only feet away! Undoubtedly, their boisterous excitement must have started to give way to a bit of fear as they were now seeing the violent waves pounding against the shoreline with no recognizable tempo or shape.

The rain and wind seemed at a fevered pitch enlivening all imagination and thrill mixing with their apprehension. Not even a flock of seagulls could be seen flying about looking for their next meal over the water's surface. Instinctively sensing the danger, these birds had already taken shelter from the storm while the menacing waves amplified their grappling and gnawing at everything in its path.

It quickly became obvious that this wouldn't be such a good idea after all. Two of the friends, Chris and Mark, shook their heads and said "No way!" They weren't even taking any chances with their boogie boards on the shoreline waves. Instead, they watched from a distance as the other two pointed their surfboards out to sea.

Jaren and his other friend, Jesse, were undeterred. Here they were – blazing with their invincible spirits and the brass of youth – as they ran headlong into the surf with their surfboards darting through the oncoming waves. Each was as determined as the other to get out past the breakwater.

Jaren paddled outward in hopes of catching the first wave and riding it all the way back to shore like he had done so many times before. But this time, his paddling was met with a pushback he had never before experienced. He was caught off guard at what was quickly to become a surfer's nightmare.

He plunged on ahead with his 6-foot-1-inch board, duck-diving under each advancing wave. As soon as he made it past the breakers, he tried to catch his breath. Looking back at his friends on shore, he tried to paddle back in hopes of catching the next wave, but the current was stronger than he expected, and he found himself being sucked out to sea. It felt as though with all his effort, he was only going backwards. He was soon swept hundreds of yards away from the shore. Jesse had caught a wave and made it back to shore. Now all three friends stood together looking fearfully out at Jaren as he helplessly drifted farther from sight into the darkness of the stormy sunset.

Night time was setting in as these three remaining friends scrambled back over the concrete wall in panic to a pay phone, dialing 911 for help.

Jesse would later recall that they could see Jaren waving for help as he drifted out of sight. They couldn't hear him shouting at the top of his lungs through the clashing tempest of the storm. He was soon enveloped within the darkness of the storm-tossed sea. All the while, I, his mother, had no idea what was happening to my boy. I wouldn't know what was happening until three or four hours later that evening.

I did not know he had even headed out to the beach after school. I was at work and thought all was well. Oh how wrong I was!

Chapter Five

His Ordeal Begins

J aren's words:

    My surfing sessions were usually brief, no more than an hour or so, because at this time of year the sun sets around 5:30 PM. Although I had done this many times before, I had no idea just how different this surf session would turn out to be.

    Faria Point is a favorite surf spot for my friends and me to surf. It is a long right-hand point that offers a long ride and a few different areas to take off from. The waves aren't as perfect as the waves out of Rincon just north a few miles, but there are usually fewer crowds which results in a more enjoyable experience.

    The point is lined with beautiful beach homes that sit about eight feet up from the shore and are protected from the erosive surf by a long concrete seawall. At low tide, it is possible to walk along the beach between the water and the seawall which allows a surfer to get in and out of the water anywhere along the point. However, most of the time the surge of the waves splashes up against the seawall which makes entry and exit to and from the water more challenging.

When we arrived at Faria that fateful day in December, I remember feeling a certain amount of nerves. The ocean has so many personalities. It can be very intimidating, and it can also be very ominous. Sometimes it seems to be saying, "Come get in and enjoy me." Other times it's saying, "Stay away from me because I am angry, dangerous and will destroy anything in my path." That particular day it was somewhere in between. If I had shown up by myself, it would have been an easy decision not to paddle out. When you have friends around it's so much easier to talk yourself into doing stupid things. And no sixteen-year-old wants to appear weak to his friends.

Two of the guys with us didn't surf so they stayed on the beach. Come to think of it, I'm not quite sure why they wanted to go to the beach that day anyway - even with their boogie boards. My best friend, Jesse, and I put on our wetsuits and walked down to the edge of the shore with our boards. I remember standing on the shore and observing the waves while I zipped up my suit and put on my leash. There was nobody else in the water which is rare for Faria and probably should have been taken as a warning not to go out.

The waves didn't look particularly large but it's hard to gauge when you don't have a human reference in the water to compare the waves with. I do remember the texture of the water wasn't smooth but rather choppy and lumpy from all the recent storm activity of the day. Jesse was a more confident surfer than myself, and I'm sure he had his reservations about going out as well. Nevertheless, we decided to go out and get a wave, maybe two, and come back in. Afterall, we only had about an hour of sunlight left. What could possibly go wrong?

As soon as you hit the water, your senses become more acute. Your bare feet feel pathetically vulnerable to the sharp rocks and barnacles as you wade through the shallows. You can feel the biting chill of the cold Pacific Ocean penetrating your wetsuit. As you begin paddling against the incoming surges of water, you are reminded of the great power that the ocean possesses. Even the smell of the ocean takes you over as it enters your sinuses with every dunk of the head.

Even though it wasn't discussed prior to paddling out, I believe Jesse and I both quickly realized upon feeling the ferocity in the water that we would use the buddy system and try and keep an eye on each other. However, this was easier said than done. We were like two specks in a very large playing field. The moving water pulled us in different directions as we put our heads down and paddled vigorously towards the horizon, trying to break through the imposing surf.

Paddling out through large surf is never easy. The waves can be relentless, and you can exert a massive amount of energy trying to paddle and duck dive through the oncoming waves. As soon as you think you have made it out, you are often caught off guard by another set of waves breaking even further out, and the cycle continues.

I remember feeling like I may not make it out and considered calling it quits. By this time, Jesse and I had been separated by some distance and communication wasn't possible. If I remember correctly, he had caught a wave and was now quite a way down the point. It was starting to get dusky, which usually indicates the end of a surf session. Right about this time the largest set of waves I had yet encountered appeared on the horizon. There are two options available in this situation. (1) Turn around and ride a wall of whitewater into the beach, or (2) paddle as hard as you can and hope to get under it before it breaks and unloads all its might on you.

As a surfer, I was programmed to go for option (2), because if you don't make it out beyond the set of waves, you don't catch a wave to surf. In a sense, it is failure. Riding in on the whitewater in the prone position on your board is no way to end a session. So, I continued to paddle toward the horizon as hard as I could.

I was barely making it over one wave when the next one in line would force me to paddle out even further. After what seemed like a ten-wave set, I finally found myself outside of where the waves were breaking and was able to catch my breath. This was great, but there was one major problem. The sun had set, and it was getting dark, fast. Not only was it getting dark, but I was suddenly frozen. Not from the cold temperature, but from panic. I didn't know what to do. I knew what I wanted to do and that was to get back to land as soon as possible. However, the recent realization of how big the surf actually was had me petrified of paddling in through the impact zone toward the safety of the beach. So, in a situation that called for quick decision making, I sat there and thought instead. This ended up being my greatest mistake.

Chapter Six

The Serenade of Mother Nature's Storm

With no idea whatsoever that Jaren was at that very moment, struggling against the waves in the storm, I was enjoying what had started out as a gentle pitter patter of the rain. As the hours of the afternoon continued, the storm grew with intensity. This was turning out to be the storm that the weather forecasters had predicted it to be!

The parched ground had become so dry that it didn't have a chance for the rainwater to sink in, causing low-lying areas to begin flooding. Sloping streets now looked like little rivers cascading down the curbsides. The wind had become more forceful and louder. There was excitement in the air with this storm, and everyone was enjoying the fulfillment of the forecasted rainstorm!

Making my way south from Ventura to Camarillo with my co-worker, rain was now coming down in sheets. Even the windshield wipers couldn't keep my windshield clear, and visibility was minimal. I was on the same 101 Freeway that Jaren had been on about an hour earlier. He was headed north, and I headed south in the opposite direction.

My co-worker and I laughed and joked about the torrents of rain as we seemed to hydroplane a couple of times through the standing water collecting on the freeway surface. We hadn't seen rain like this in such a long time and were enjoying every explosive drop of it. It sounded as though we were in a tin can being pelted with rocks. We laughed about the wind, and how it felt like we were in some kind of *The Wizard Of Oz* movie. We were expecting at any time to see something come flying through the air at us. Unable to contain ourselves from laughter, we then burst out singing "Follow the Yellow Brick Road" in our animated munchkin voices. We were giddy and having the time of our lives. But we were also very naïve about the power of this storm.

It still haunts me to this day that while I was reveling in the storm and being so silly and carefree about it, my son was out there in an unforgiving ocean, struggling with all his might to survive because of that very same storm.

Passing through the entrance gate of the Spanish Hills Country Club and finding a parking spot, I now gave out a loud "ONE! TWO! THREE! GO!" We leaped out of the car and ran as quickly as we could to the entrance. Our clothing felt more like wet paper towels clinging to us before we had a chance to get inside. But who cared? Mother Nature was on full display in all her glory, and we were loving it! Yet to my horror and enormous guilt, I would a few hours later learn that while I had been enjoying a night of dining and networking with my associates, my son had already been lost at sea for more than four hours!

Chapter Seven

Why is Becky Standing in the Rain at the Gate?

I t had been an enjoyable evening with great food and discussion. After the meeting was over and all of us said our goodbyes, we all darted back to our own cars, once again getting soaked to the bone. The rain hadn't let up – it seemed to be coming down even harder.

Back in my car, again completely drenched, my coworker and I burst out laughing at how funny we all must have looked running for the shelter of our cars. I remember that what had earlier been the remaining traces of my carefully applied mascara was now trickling down my cheeks. Still laughing, I started the car engine and headed through the maze of the parking lot and toward the exit gate.

Driving nearer to the exit gate I saw two rain-soaked figures huddled together which struck me as quite odd. This sight didn't make any sense given the pouring rain and darkness of the night. I was a bit apprehensive as I pulled closer to see who these two figures could be. *Maybe homeless people looking for help*, I thought to myself. I was stunned at the unmistakable realization that one of these rain-soaked figures was my daughter, Becky. I hurried my car over to them and saw that Ruth, a neighbor, was by her side. Their expressions were drawn in worry, and my stomach began to twist as I rolled down my car window. "What are you doing here?" I asked.

With a quivering voice that could only mean trouble, the only word Becky could utter was "Mom." In that instant and sound of her voice, I knew that something terrible had happened. My heart stopped as Ruth chimed in, "There's been a problem with Jaren." Leading me to the thought of *Oh no! He's broken his leg on his skateboard.* Now giving way to the tremendous feeling of a dagger ripping through my heart, she continued with the words, "He's gone surfing and we can't find him."

Unable to process what I was hearing, my mind quickly spiraled into a place of chaos, rendering me unable to think rationally. Enormous feelings of guilt flashed through my mind. I had been enjoying a nice dinner meeting at a country club with the wonderful backdrop sounds of rain pounding on the rooftop, while my son was lost at sea and fighting for his life!

I ordered my co-worker out of my car and to find another ride home. With Becky now in his seat, we raced over to the house that was by now the epicenter of commotion.

Chapter Eight

Turn It Off!

I wasn't prepared for what I found upon entering the front door of the house. The living room was filled with my children's teenage friends gathered around the blaring TV, watching the rain-soaked reporters on the shore continue to describe the events surrounding Jaren's disappearance and that in fact, he was lost at sea. Hearing his name echoing on the TV, while the ticker tape at the bottom of the screen flashed his tragic news, was more than I could take. "Turn it off!" I shouted.

Trying to collect my thoughts was impossible. My ex-husband, Doug, was already out there searching for our son. He had scrambled out the door to the beach when he heard the news of Jaren being pulled out to sea.

It was dinner time when Jesse and his father, Ron, had arrived at the house with the news of them going surfing and that Jaren was unable to make it back to shore. At this, Doug threw down his fork, grabbed his car keys and was out of sight in no time, speeding north on the 101 Freeway towards Pitas Point not knowing what to expect.

Shortly after my arrival at the house, Doug called from a beach pay phone. We were both in a state of shock and grappled to make sense of the situation. He thought it best that I stay at the house with the girls and told me not to come out there. But of course, I wouldn't stay behind. Knowing Melissa and Becky would be okay, I told him I would be out there as quickly as I could get to my apartment and change my clothes.

After hanging up, my first thought was to call my local church leader, Bishop Martin. Though technically he was no longer my bishop, I had known him for many years and had always trusted him for his kind words of wisdom and his spiritual strengths. He was always like a beacon of light to me. I didn't know what he could possibly tell me at a time like this, but I felt strongly that I should make the call.

With trembling fingers, I dialed his number. The phone rang only a couple of times, but it felt like an eternity before there was an answer on the other end. When he finally answered, I blurted out, "Bishop, Jaren went surfing and now we can't find him!" Without any hesitation, he calmly spoke, "Sister, your son is going to be okay." My immediate thought was, *WHAT?!* These weren't the words I was expecting to hear. But his reassuring voice gave me a sense of calm, and in the most fleeting moment, I wasn't afraid.

Understandably, many might question and even doubt the peace that I felt, but when he said those words, I had the immediate sense of peace throughout my whole body. There seemed to be a higher power communicating to me through his words that Jaren wasn't lost in God's eyes nor would he be left to himself to survive such a storm as this. It was as though a small window of light opened within my soul.

But, almost as quickly as that window had opened, the door of peace immediately slammed shut against my mind, leaving me seized upon with greater feelings of doubt and fear. I, of all people, didn't feel worthy of that incomprehensible peace I was given in that brief phone conversation with Bishop Martin. But his words were the strength I would so desperately cling to during the hours ahead as the uncertainty and anguish lingered on throughout that late night and early morning hours of the next day. Oh, how I wanted to believe that Jaren would really be okay when I hung up the phone. But my faith was weak, and all I knew about past stories of this nature never had a good ending.

Admittedly any sense of my faith quickly collapsed under the weight of my excruciating worry. I wanted to be able to find even a particle of faith and hope – the kind I had been taught about all my life or even felt on my own in quiet moments as a little girl. I wanted to believe that God really was in the details at that very moment. But the voices in my head were already gathering in strength and shouting that faith and hope, or even prayer, would not save my son.

Even so, my desire to believe, weak as it was, stood against or perhaps among those competing voices, and I prayed more earnestly that the elements of the storm would not harm my son. I desperately pled that Jaren would be given the strength to hold on to his surfboard and hold on to his own ability to muster any of his own hope and faith, no matter what he was facing out there in the storm-tossed sea. I asked God to assure Jaren that he wasn't alone in his struggle.

With such tearful pleadings, I was praying more intently that the elements of the storm would not harm my son. I hoped for him to feel that a greater power would be there to help him navigate whatever it was he would face while all attempts to find him were being done.

My heart felt peace for a very brief moment, but once again I was floundering in my struggle to collect my thoughts. Even more importantly, to grasp as tight as I could to my faith. I wanted to help Melissa and Becky find their faith and hope that he could survive this terrible storm and come out of it unharmed.

Taking them to the covered backyard patio away from all the confusion inside the house, we huddled together under the clattering noise of the rain. I tearfully pleaded with God to protect Jaren and bring him back home. I acknowledged that I had no doubt that God knew where he was. I affirmed what Bishop Martin had said to me minutes earlier and that I believed his words. There was part of me that believed God could and would save my son.

I hesitate to admit this, but in a way, I may have sounded like I was demanding a miracle. That's not the case. I only wanted God to know I did believe He is over all things in spite of the life I had been living. I had turned away from religion some years before this and was no longer living the life that I knew I should be living. Now I would have to honestly face God in all my unworthiness as I pleaded for His divine help.

My common sense and the severity of the storm coupled with the fact that he had already been lost for over four hours pointed to a much different outcome. Oh how I pleaded that Jaren would be protected, that he would be able to hold onto his surfboard and be found alive! Now there were more tears streaming down our cheeks than there were rain drops pounding on the patio's metal roof.

We were pleading for a miracle, and we wanted to believe. I felt a huge weight of responsibility to be an example of courage and strength for my daughters in those prayerful moments. They were scared, but I didn't want them to give up hope. I didn't want to give in to the fear. I wanted my girls to trust that God was over all, come what may.

I can't remember everything about that prayer except for the anguish in our hearts knowing he was out there in that explosive ocean alone, contending with the elements. Would God bring him safely back to shore? All logic shouted with a resounding NO! Yet we wanted to believe!

Chapter Nine

At the Shore

I left my daughters in the safety of the house, surrounded by protectors and comforters, and was now heading north towards Ventura on the 101 Freeway to my apartment. The rain was still coming down in sheets. Just as they had hours earlier, the windshield wipers couldn't keep up with rain and the explosive pelting of rain drops. This time there was no laughter, only fear and apprehension. I couldn't get to my apartment quick enough to change and head further up the coast to where Jaren was last seen.

While continuing up HWY 101, I could see that the whole coastline seemed to be lit up with search lights facing out to sea. My heart sank again with fear. My grip on the car door handle tightened as I stepped out into the crowded Faria Beach Campground. The ocean air was thicker than usual with the scent of salt and my hair whipped across my face leaving its taste upon my lips. My eyes were immediately met with dark silhouetted bodies of people, young and old, scattered along the coastline. They were flickering in and out of the bright glare of search lights facing towards the ocean. By now, owners of their beach front properties also had their surroundings lit up in a futile yet compassionate effort to illuminate past the breakwaters of the shore. It was immediately clear to me that hundreds of people had come from all over Ventura County to help search for Jaren. With emotions already welling up inside, I could hardly hold back a new flood of tears. Before me was a multitude of true humanity and love in this time of my great need.

Once parked and out of my car, I was directly swooped upon by a blur of media reporters with their glaring lights and rain gear, each jockeying for my attention. Trying to protect my eyes from the glare, I felt as if I were under attack from their barrage of questions. I quickly became agitated at what seemed like the most insensitive questions – "Are you worried about your son? Does he have much experience surfing? What will you do when you find him?" – questions that felt more like salt to a wound. Believe me. You *never* want to ask a mother what she is feeling at a time like that. I had zero patience or intention of answering their rapid-fire questions. There was no time to waste in front of their cameras and microphones. I scattered them off like shewing a flock of seagulls away from a picnic blanket on the beach. They disbursed without fanfare back into the darkness of the storm.

Finding myself at a command post of first responders, I was able to catch up with Doug, who forty-five minutes earlier had encouraged me to stay with the girls. Now I was by his side searching for our son.

As the media again focused their attention on us, it was clear that Doug was also in no mood for them. The clamor of their presence, muted by noise and confusion with the backdrop of howling wind and rain, made it seem more like a "made for TV" drama. In their shouted outbursts of questions, they quickly became more like sharks in a feeding frenzy as they swirled around us. My mind turned towards the sharks in the ocean, causing every imaginable horror to burst through new, uncharted corners of my mind. The panic in my chest grew as I desperately wanted to believe my son would survive.

Everything around us was so surreal. I felt myself begin to crumble as I could only shudder under the weight of the reality of our situation. I wanted to believe this was a nightmare and wake up.

Though each reporter seemed relentless at trying to get a good story, they made one final attempt at Doug and me. Our actions made it very clear – we had nothing to say to them! Finding Jaren was our only focus.

This was the last I saw or took notice of them. I didn't know or care if they stayed during the long hours ahead – so long as they stayed away from me.

My memory fell back to a few years earlier. I had read about a young couple who had gone kayaking to the Channel Islands. It had been a beautiful sunny day, however, they never returned to their homes that night. Days later, only one of the kayaks was found. There were bite marks and a large gap on the side, believed to be from a great white shark. Sadly, their bodies were never found.

I also thought about the shark attacks in recent years just off the coast. It's said that because of the black wetsuits worn by surfers, sharks often mistake them for seals and attack. All these horrific thoughts charged through my mind, creating its own feeding frenzy of imaginations and fear of Jaren's fate. Crying out in horror, I begged for God's intervention on Jaren's behalf to keep the sharks from swimming anywhere near him.

Where is he?! I couldn't see anything but black. There were no stars or moon to light the ocean's surface. My eyes strained to see, but there was only thick blackness and tumultuous noise everywhere.

I followed Doug back to the command post where I was introduced to a local sheriff. His demeanor was grim as he tried to calmly brief us on all the search efforts being made and any status of Jaren's possible whereabouts they might have up to that point. Four hours had already elapsed, and a Coast Guard ship had finally been dispatched from Channel Islands Harbor a few miles south. The crew hadn't been able to set out any earlier because of the intensity of the waves which could capsize the ship, putting the crew in danger. With the impatience of a frightened mother, this seemed like too little of an effort. Looking back on that night, it was obvious that I wasn't thinking about the safety of others. I regret that now, but at the time, the only thing I could think about was Jaren's safe return. I demanded to know about a search and rescue helicopter. Was it hovering over the ocean searching for my son? Surely, it must have been dispatched hours ago once the 911 call had come through.

So many times, before this night, I had seen the same helicopter hovering in the sky but had paid little attention as to why it was there or who the search was for. I had always thought they were just out looking for some "bad guy." But this night was different.

The sheriff shook his head telling me it would be too dangerous for a helicopter to fly because of the low visibility and wind shears. My inability to think logically gave way, and I yelled out, "That's my son out there! You've got to send that helicopter out!"

Knowing the helicopter could not go out in that storm magnified my fear. It was alarming how quickly I was losing my grip on being able to reason with the situation. I had never been so scared as I was then.

"Your son's going to be okay." My bishop's assurance once again tried to find its voice in my clouded mind. However, shouts of a different outcome quickly silenced any feelings of comfort or hope. Faith was already seeming more like a fairytale. I was struggling to believe, even though I couldn't deny the fleeting moments of peace and assurance I had felt earlier as I gathered my daughters together to pray for Jaren.

Recognizing my great alarm and panic, the sheriff did all he could to reassure me that if the winds let up, the helicopter would be dispatched and that all possible rescue efforts were being made. I wanted to believe, but I wanted more help there on the water. I wanted the National Guard!

Police cars, fire trucks and ambulances were everywhere. I was having to face the reality that Jaren's situation was larger than all of us combined.

The sheriff tried his best to calm me by telling both me and Doug that the best thing we could hope for now would be that Jaren's surfboard wouldn't be found along the shore. Hopefully this would mean that he was still on it and above water. Not a whole lot of encouragement, but it was the best he could give right then. I'm sure his view of the outcome was bleak. But it gave a faint spark to the weakening light of my faith, and I prayed that Jaren would be able to hold on to his surfboard.

I was amazed at all the people who had come to help in the search efforts. People I didn't even know had come from all around. They had seen Jaren's story on the TV or heard it on the radio. My mother had also been one of those to see it on the TV. She had frantically called just before I had left for the beach. Now she, along with other family members and friends, was combing the shoreline in a desperate search for a sixteen-year-old boy. Still more people continued to gather wanting to help find him. Some came with flashlights, food, and blankets. I sensed the feeling that everyone involved felt as if he could have been one of their own. A son, brother, or friend. They were all gathered in a single cause – to help find my son. Now more than ever, hope filled my heart as I saw firsthand the charity and humanity of others.

Doug and I made our way out to the first boulders of a jetty in hopes of getting a glimpse of Jaren. A wave broke directly in front of us, so we scrambled back to safer ground on shore. Little did we know, Jaren was actually within sight. Because of the rain, wind, and darkness, we weren't able to see or hear him. Jaren would later recall seeing us standing on the shore with the lights from the Faria beach store behind. He recognized the dark shadow to be his father on the distant shoreline and yelled out, but he quickly realized he couldn't be seen or heard. How his heart must have sunk at that moment.

***

He would later recall:

The lights inside the houses along the point were now on, and it was quickly transitioning from dusk to darkness. I could faintly see my friends on the beach, including Jesse with his surfboard. Seeing Jesse on the beach instantly made the situation worse because I now knew that I was alone out there on the water. They were waving their arms at me, and I was waving mine back at them. For the moment I still had hope because it seemed they could at least see me, and I could see them. I could almost hear them saying to each other, "What the heck is he doing? Why isn't he paddling in?" I sat there staring at them while I assessed my situation. I think I was in some kind of denial about how serious the situation would be if I didn't get back to the beach soon.

As I sat there, the last bit of light in the sky eventually vanished. This is when the real panic set in. I was in a cold, stormy ocean alone in complete darkness. It was scary enough before when I could see the waves coming, but now I could not. The only way to ensure I didn't get caught by a rogue set of waves was to paddle way out where the waves couldn't possibly break. When a large swell is in the water the waves break further out to sea than they normally do. So I paddled out a good distance.

Now I was further away from shore which made me feel even more isolated. I was far from shore and drifting slowly to the north. I could see that I was north of the point now and assumed my friends no longer knew where I was. It would be impossible for anybody to track me considering

I was wearing a black wetsuit at night. After a few desperate screaming fits, I eventually decided it was useless to yell. The roar of the large waves breaking would drown out any noise I made, especially considering how far away from shore I was.

At some point the weather began to turn for the worse. Rain started falling and a strong south wind picked up, making the ocean very choppy and textured. The strong winds coupled with the ocean current would eventually push me nearly a mile north of Faria. I was very familiar with the area, and this was not where I wanted to be.

The coast north of Faria provided no safe place to come ashore. The storm driven waves were crashing violently against a sea wall that consisted of large boulders piled up on the sand. This rock wall stretched for about a mile and half north of Faria. Eventually I came to the conclusion that my best chances to safely get ashore would be in the bay just south of Faria. This bay is somewhat sheltered by Faria Point from the larger surf. Waves break at the top of the point and tend to taper off as they get into the bay. However, to get to this bay I would need to paddle a mile against the wind and current. So, I began paddling. Then paddled and paddled and paddled some more. After that I paddled even more. Paddling against a strong current is like walking on a treadmill. Your arms are moving a lot, but you're not really going anywhere.

At this point in the story, my reference of time becomes very unclear. I suppose I had a lot of adrenaline pumping throughout my body as my natural instinct to survive took over. I recall thinking my friends were probably still on the beach waiting for me to come ashore. Little did I know several hours had passed, and I was now classified as a bona fide missing person lost at sea.

It is truly remarkable how time didn't seem to exist out there. It's as if I was so hyper focused on getting out of the ocean that the only indication that time had elapsed was the feeling of fatigue and hunger. I didn't know that hours were ticking by like minutes. I didn't know my whole family was aware I never came in from my surf and were now looking for me up and down the coast. I didn't know my friends were going to bed that night thinking they would never see me again. I didn't know the Coast Guard had been alerted. I remember seeing numerous emergency vehicles going up and down the highway along the coast and wondering what was going on, not knowing they were looking for me. Evidently the Coast Guard was unable to dispatch a helicopter to look for me due to the severity of the winds that night.

Chapter Ten

The Night Lingers On

Time plodded on with no sight of Jaren or his surfboard and still the helicopter could not be dispatched. I saw many more people who came to search through the buffeting wind, in their rain-drenched clothing. These figures were silhouetted against the glaring search lights. They were scattered up and down the coastline. Each still hoping for the miracle that seemed so hopeless.

Many around me were becoming very concerned. Well-meaning people tried to console me but could not. I needed to be alone and began to wander along the shoreline, trying to gather my thoughts while straining my eyes out into the darkness hoping for any sight of my son.

Everywhere I looked, I was met with gloomy darkness shrouded with the blur of the pouring rain. It was almost impossible to see past the gray froth of breaking waves on shore. Each crashing wave filled me with increasing panic and a sense of doom. Against all my willingness to acknowledge it, I was becoming more aware of just how precarious any rescue attempts were at that point. I knew the storm was fierce, and I was soaked. I needed to be able to see flashes of the searchlights from the Coast Guard out there. But I couldn't see anything! And even worse, I couldn't hear any audible sounds of their engine.

The wind was now blowing with greater strength. Everything seemed to take on a distorted life form of its own. I felt like I was standing on the outskirts of a tornado trying to make sense of chaos in every direction, as all possible efforts were being made to find and save Jaren. There were masses of people and rescue equipment on shore, yet Jaren was still alone to fight for himself off shore.

I struggled to comprehend what Jaren was up against. How far had he been taken out to sea? How large were the waves that he was contending with? I knew these waves were huge by their deafening sounds as they slammed onto shore. But what would he be facing out there all alone in that stormy sea, while I was wandering safely on shore surrounded by people?

These were the kind of waves I had once loved watching off the end of the pier as they would roll closer and finally burst through the planks and into the air. But I now found myself screaming at the top of my lungs for the waves to "STOP!"

Knowing my son was out there alone, and we were all together safe on shore, was unbearable. I could only continue pleading in my heart that Jaren would be able to have the endurance he needed to hold on to the safety of his surfboard and not give up. With what little faith or even hope I could find, I prayed that God would surround Jaren with all of

His search and rescue team – the angels – and bring him safely back to shore.

My mother, Joy, and sister, Cindy, along with our good friend, Lori, found me and were my blanket of comfort. Even though my mom was no more consolable than I was, I needed her there. Each had raced out the moment they heard the news. Mom's fear of Jaren's certain doom had struck her with unbearable dread. To this day, she speaks of the fear she felt as she watched the fury of the ocean, knowing that one of her grandsons was out there somewhere in the angry ocean. She feared for the worst. I was fighting the same bouts of fear and tearful outbursts. Yet I needed my mother and all of us to cling to our faith in God as impossible as the situation was. He was our only hope for Jaren.

Even though I was trying to be strong for my mother, I couldn't hide the fact that I felt more like a frightened little child myself standing by her side. My life as a child flashed before my eyes taking me to a time when I was a little girl and my mother was my protector. Now all these years later, I was a mother and couldn't protect my own son from this terrible storm. My mind began to spiral in anxiety for Jaren's welfare.

Once again, I needed to pull myself back together. The words "your son's going to be okay" were snuffed out by the tormenting shouts in my mind, and my faith felt like foolishness. Was I naïve to hang on to such hope? I stood at the water's edge. A much more ominous story was playing out there. Could I not see reality before my own eyes?

Chapter Eleven

One Quarter of the Pier is Destroyed

By now, Jared, a close family friend and some of the other kids, had left our house of confusion and took it upon themselves to drive out to the Ventura pier in hopes of spotting Jaren. The gate of the pier had been closed due to the severity of the storm. The gate itself isn't high and can easily be climbed over. So over they went. As they ran across the edge of the pier, they were hit by the waves coming up from beneath the planks. By this time the pier was already rocking back and forth while they made their way out to the farthest point of the pier. As teenage kids can be, I'm sure they didn't even give it a thought that they could be putting themselves in danger. But Jaren was their friend, and they were undeterred, wanting to help find any sign of him.

Squinting against the dark and rain, they now found themselves enveloped in the thick darkness offshore. The pier began to rock violently, and they sensed their own danger as a sudden crackling and crumbling noise groaned beneath their feet. Fearing for their lives, they knew they needed to get off that pier as quickly as they could because it was clearly rupturing beneath them.

It would be reported the next day that a quarter of the pier was destroyed that night, sustaining $1.5 million in damage. Had they not hurried off the pier, they would have inevitably lost their lives in the debris and destruction of the once longest wooden pier on the whole West Coast of the Pacific Ocean. With adrenaline pumping, they then joined the rest of the searchers on the safety of the shore.

Minutes seemed like hours. Everything was in slow motion. I felt a tugging at my soul that I had a responsibility to hold on to the words of Bishop Martin, "Your son's going to be okay." I needed to try harder to keep my focus on my faith in God and my hope that He would save Jaren from this storm, even as unlikely as everything dictated. There were so many conflicting feelings by now, and the internal shouts of reason were beginning to convince me that I was losing my mind and telling me that there would be no fairytale ending to this story. I fought back against those feelings. I knew full well that my mind was not in any fairytale state of thinking. I only wanted to believe that God was over all. I was hanging by a thread onto Bishop Martin's words of comfort.

Had he not told me those exact words, my expectations would have been disastrous. But I needed to believe! It was the only thread of hope that I could hold on to, and I could only hope his words of confidence would somehow carry through to Jaren.

Doug and I were moved with the mobile emergency search and rescue command post to another location about a mile south of the original place. Still no word of finding Jaren and no sightings of his surfboard. The fact that there wasn't any sign of Jaren's surfboard was supposed to be comforting news, but I found very little comfort in it. Everything was looking and sounding the same wherever we went, and there was still no Jaren to be found.

Again, the sheriff continued to patiently reaffirm that all possible rescue efforts were still being employed. Yet, for me, it still wasn't enough and his words felt meaningless. Where was my faith and hope to be found now?

Chapter Twelve

My Personal Storm

"Where is my son?" I cried out in utter despair. He had vanished from my life in the darkness of the storm-tossed ocean. The horrific hours crawled on with no sight of him. There was no sign of the storm's intent of bringing her violent waves to a calm.

"My son! Where are you? Why can't I see you?" I felt like the ocean laughed as I crumbled before the water's edge pleading her to not take him away from me. "Why would you harm my son?" My heart didn't understand, and my mind was unable to grasp the gravity of this situation. All was dark. All was dire! I tried to keep the shattering pieces of my soul from spilling onto the wet sand before me. Every corner of my mind was chaotic with the shouts of voices taunting me that I would never again see my son alive. "STOP!" I shouted back! I spiraled to an unrecognizable place in my mind. I had never been there before, and I was afraid.

I was immediately struck as I realized there were now two storms. My son was swept out to sea in this vicious rain storm, fighting for his life, and I was in an internal storm fighting for clarity as I tried to hold on to the courage that I might be worthy of his safe return.

But wait a second. Worthy? Why should his deliverance be determined upon my worthiness? Do I hold his destiny in my hands? No! Could I believe that God would take him from me because I was unworthy of miracles? What kind of God was I creating in my bruised and tortured mind?

The God I believe in is not a cruel God, intent on punishing me by purposely allowing my son to be swept out to sea, never to be found. Such thoughts would only further prove my lack of understanding of God's unwavering love for the Sinner as well as the Innocent.

I wanted to believe He heard my pleadings and that He tenderly wanted me to feel His care and concern. I wanted to believe that He, too, was with Jaren, holding him from harm's evil grip.

For years I had shut my ears to God because I was afraid to hear. I had closed my eyes because I was afraid to see. I ran and continued to run, because I was afraid to be found. I became bitter within my own soul, allowing past injustices and personal mistakes to lead me to believe that I was not worthy. And now I found myself on a dark, cold shore fighting two very real storms, forced to choose definitively between faith and fear.

Before this particular night, I had been awoken almost every night from my sleep, hearing my name. The voice was so quiet and gentle, but it had the power to penetrate and wake me from a sound sleep. The voice would say, "Cheri, I haven't forgotten you. Why are you running from me? My arms are open. Let me heal your hurts and mistakes. Let me breathe new life into your soul and set you back on your path, that you too may also be rescued." The inner storm on both fronts continued throughout the hours as we desperately searched for my son.

My pleadings for Jaren's safety intensified as the search parties started to dwindle. I prayed that my son would hear and recognize that same gentle voice that I had so many times ignored. I wanted him to know that he was not alone out there. I needed him to hold onto his own faith while I struggled to remain vigilant on shore trying to grasp onto the greater faith I once had. Following the example of my mother, I had taught each of my children to pray from a very early age. I hoped Jaren did believe God was aware of him and was also praying.

That night, I knew what it felt like to be a loving and concerned parent, physically separated from my child and unable to make him hear and see me, and all the while desperate that he would have his own faith in my love and desire for him to return safely to my arms. In subtle but profound ways, I could see what my Father in Heaven also felt for me, mirrored in my own personal, stormy life.

Chapter Thirteen

Everyone is Doing All They Can

The sheriff continued to try to reassure Doug and me by telling us that the best thing we could still hope for at that moment was that Jaren's surfboard or fragments of it wouldn't be found washing up on shore. Hopefully this would mean he was still on it and above water. By now his words were beginning to sound like a broken record. I believe the sheriff was running out of positive scenarios himself. He must have been thinking there would be no miracles. Yet, it was his task to try keeping two scared parents as calm as possible. He had known of so many other fates in his career and his somber mannerisms were a telltale sign of his uncertainty.

I'm sure his view of the outcome was becoming bleaker with every passing hour. But for me, it gave a spark to the tiny, flickering light of my faith.

How hard it must have been for him trying to keep me calm while maybe thinking of his own son safely at home, tucked into his own bed. Did he think to pray for my son? I was hoping so.

Time felt at a standstill, while visions of my son's life were playing through my mind like a movie. I saw visions of the first time I held my newborn baby boy in my arms. I remembered the sound of his cry as he took his first breath of life. I had promised God I would take good care of him and protect him. I didn't want this fierce storm at sea to be the cause of his last breath. I was reliving each moment of his life as they played vividly before my eyes. I wanted to scream and make it all stop. But the memories kept racing through every corner of my mind along with deepening feelings of guilt and regret.

I remembered when he was about three years old, we had taken a little family excursion to another pier in Santa Barbara. There was a wide pipe leading from offshore into the harbor. I remembered his cute little lisp as he asked, "Is that the hose Heavenly Father uses to fill the ocean?" As every detail of this memory played out with greater clarity, I began to cry even harder and wished so much I could find a way to drain the ocean that night.

By now, it had been over six hours since Jaren was last seen by his friends. Blaring logic shouted what the inevitable must be. I was in my lowest moments, and my faith quickly gave way to despair.

Pushing against my despair was a feeling that felt like a little trickle of light entering my mind. I felt a calm sensation gently descend upon me like a warm blanket. Pushing back against all the frantic voices in my mind,

I was once again hearing the words of Bishop Martin: "Your son's going to be okay."

The frantic voices fought back, but there was an unmistakable peace that seemed to bring a calm to my tortured mind. Light illuminated where darkness once was. "Your son's going to be okay" rang out with clarity and peace. It spoke in gentle but strong power – unlike the frantic screams of what had been clouding my ability to trust in the power of miracles. Could what Bishop Martin had told me earlier really be God's intended outcome and miracle for Jaren?

I thought I had the faith that he would be spared. But I also thought of the countless stories of people, young and old who had been lost at sea. Whether by boating accident, shark attack or swimming too far from the shoreline and ultimately drowning. Who was I to expect a miraculous end to Jaren's fate at sea when so many others had suffered the grief and loss of a loved one? Now like many others before, Jaren's situation was looking hopeless without the promise of a happy ending.

Chapter Fourteen

Finding Hope in the Storm

L ike the flaxen threads of a cord weaving its way through my mind, I felt the battle of conflicting thoughts ramp up with each woven thread of calamity against calm. All rationale and hope battled one against the other to win. Navigating through these opposing thoughts in my mind was becoming almost impossible. I was in shock and disbelief. I feared I would never see my son again. But without logical explanation during the war of outcomes in my mind, there continued to be a prevailing reassurance, telling me that my son would be okay.

By now, I found myself needing to be alone again. Although I was filled with gratitude for everyone who had come to our aid, I felt like I couldn't breathe. The weight of the thick, salty air in the atmosphere felt as though it had penetrated every space in my clouded mind. The thrashing sounds of the waves roaring against the shore seemed to mimic the erratic heartbeat within me. I then understood what it felt like to believe my heart would burst. My hair, completely limp with the damp, salty air, mirrored my feelings of despondency. Feelings of guilt amplified while the caustic inner voices whirled around my mind like circling sharks.

In this fearful state of mind, I reflected on the hours before, when I was laughing it up with my co-worker about the rain and wind as we had driven to our meeting. Two carefree people thinking this storm was just the icing on the cake for a great dinner meeting and mingling. I had joked about not being surprised if we saw a cow flying through the air because of the wind. Everything had been comical, and I didn't think I had a care in the world. Now, all these hours later, my world was shattering like broken glass tossed against the large boulders of a shoreline jetty.

How would I ever be able to pick up all the shattered pieces of my life, when out there in the darkness a huge chunk of it was being ripped away? Those few short hours before, I was laughing and dining without a care in the world thinking Melissa, Jaren and Becky were each safely under the shelter of their father's home.

In solitude, I walked further up shore, passing between groups of people who remained looking for Jaren. Most of them didn't even know I was his mother. I felt comforted knowing that so many were still there looking for him. During my moments of searching alone, I found my mind not only ramping up with the tormenting tug-of-war of cruel shouts against my trembling whisperings of faith and hope, I found my emotional strength falter as each onslaught of dark thoughts darted against any sense of peace.

I was in a place where clinging to the slightest thread of faith or hope for Jaren's survival was nearly impossible. But in those moments a still small voice echoed the words, "Your son's going to be okay." These comforting words had power against my mental anguish and helped me see through my tear swollen eyes with a renewed sense of hope. And, even though it must have been over eight hours by now, my faith sparked just a little brighter against my doubt and fear.

Although I was wandering the shoreline by myself, I began to feel so sure there were others surrounding me, holding me up. I felt the presence of so many, and the atmosphere surrounding me was thick with an inexplicable energy.

Could it be that my grandmother who had passed away a few years before was standing by my side? I felt her presence and all of a sudden I was reminded of a time before she passed away when she had called me. She was crying because of a nightmare she had the night before. She told me she saw me drifting away from shore and yelling for help. She tried to reach out to me but couldn't. She could only watch as I drifted out of sight. It was a horrible nightmare.

Strange how her dream now reflected what was happening that very night. I felt encouragement and promptings to not give up. For some reason, I felt reassured that although Jaren was in great danger, it wouldn't have the power to take his life. I had the sure feeling that he was still holding onto his surfboard. Were there also loved ones by his side protecting him? I felt sure there were.

I thought I could see him in my mind's eye. He was being buffeted by the waves and was extremely tired and hungry. He was afraid but determined. I could see he was having a hard time staying on his surfboard, but he wasn't giving up either. My heart took courage because I knew that like me, he wasn't alone. My prayers felt heard, though I still didn't know what the final outcome would be. Would he be found by the Coast Guard? Or would he somehow make it back to shore on his own? My continued prayer for him was that he be given the strength and clarity of mind to remain strong in that terrible ocean and not let go of his surfboard.

Even after each inclination of hope, I would again second guess myself. I found myself staggering between feelings of great alarm mingled with brief moments of quietude and peace. The inner battles within my mind grew all the more difficult to navigate. I was emotionally depleted. My fears screamed out louder and louder, and I plead for this storm to cease and let us find Jaren unharmed.

It's strange that with all the battles playing out in my mind, I noticed the taste of salty tears tracing my lips as memories of a happier place and time now gave way to my thoughts and allowed the feeling of a slight smile to take shape. I found myself clinging to each memory that passed my view, wanting to be back in every moment, never to leave again.

I had failed in my marriage and because of this, for a long time I felt I had failed my children. As the salty tears streamed down my cheeks, memories began to flood my mind, but rather than torment me, I had the feeling that I *was* a good mother after all. I was reminded that although I was lost and floundering in my personal life, that didn't make me less of a mother. Melissa, Jaren and Becky were my pride and joy. Letting my own lack of self esteem and poor choices dictate my identity was my downfall. But no matter what, my children were and are my greatest joy!

Oh the good memories and moments that danced through my thoughts right then. I was taken back to a time when my three little toe-heads were always helping me with our backyard garden and raspberry patch along one side of the fence. Well, they thought they were helping. They would pick the corn at two inches; carrots never had a chance to grow more than an inch, and the radishes looked more like wispy tear drops of pink. As for the raspberries? I never harvested a full bowl. I would laugh to myself while watching them with their happy little faces and fat little hands forage for something to eat. Each would run to me with brimming smiles and show me what they had picked. Such cute little gardeners they were. And so eager to help. When dinner time came around, they were never that hungry, but I didn't care knowing they had filled themselves with good nutrition all day long.

Simpler times in life and thoughts of the children playing about within the protection of a large fenced backyard gave my mind a brief moment of peace and happiness. I reflected on times when I knew exactly where my three little ones were and that each was safe.

More memories surfaced, like when the time had come to let each practice driving my car when they got their learner's permits. Melissa was the oldest and first to drive in my little red BMW. She smashed the front parking lights out, hitting the retaining wall in a parking lot. She put her foot on the gas instead of the brakes, and we all sailed to an abrupt stop. She couldn't understand why I was laughing while our two backseat drivers, Jaren and Becky, were scolding her. To me it was just the beginning of making fun memories of learning to drive for years to come.

Now Jaren on the other hand, was another story. He said, "Check this out," and took a corner so fast and sharp, we yelled out thinking for sure the car would roll on its side. He only laughed then peeled out from the next stop sign up the street. I had to laugh then and ask if he really thought I would let him take the car on his own when he got his license. He replied. "Dude, I won't do that when you're not in the car." "Sure you won't, and stop calling me 'Dude,'" I laughed. But I really didn't mind him calling me "Dude." He was comical how he would stumble and say, "Sorry Dude,... I mean Mom... Dude. Dude...Mom." I could only laugh more.

Two years later, it was Becky's turn to learn. We were in Ventura waiting to make a left turn on a busy street, when the light turned green. Sure enough, when it did, she stepped on the gas. She didn't notice that the turn signal arrow was still red. All in the car screamed out, "BECKY!" as she pulled turned directly in front of an oncoming van. Her reply? "Well, the light was green." Luckily everything turned out okay. I burst out laughing once I knew our lives weren't over. "Pull over," I tried to say with composure, still laughing and grateful to be alive.

I wondered why the memories of my children learning to drive stood out the most. Could it have been that these memories of learning to drive were racing against the driving thoughts of doom in my mind? Perhaps it was because their learning to drive was the first time I, as their mother, really had to sit back and watch them take the wheel - leaving me a more or less helpless spectator as they navigated foreign territory. Was that not a potentially life threatening experience? And yet we took each mile, each mistake, each new turn in stride. Not only did we take it in stride, we laughed! There was joy in the journey. Even with the bumps and turns, everything worked itself out as we trusted in the learning process.

These fleeting memories were a brief shelter from the storm. I could remember how many times before, I had loved dancing along the shoreline playing "catch me if you can" with the incoming waves. Now these waves were only wretched claws darting onto shore, violently scratching and digging at anything in their path. Their thunderous pounding at my feet made me shudder, wishing I could take back all the years. I wanted to redo so many things – like spend more time with my kids instead of wasted days trying to find the perfect job or perfect relationship. I took for granted just how precious my time with each was until this terrible night - one that would change my outlook on life forever.

I had been running away from pain and disappointment in my life for many years. I made choices that I wasn't proud of. Memories of things that had happened that I couldn't control still haunted me. I had tried to fill my life and distract myself from dealing with things I didn't want to think about, but tonight, I was met with a brick wall. I knew some things needed to change in my life. This night gave me a purpose and clarity that gave me motivation I had not been able to find before. I shook my head and saved further reflection for another time. I didn't want to dwell on my own life. Tonight my only focus was that I needed to find my son.

How could I never see my son or hear his voice again? Would I ever be able to listen and watch as he so beautifully played his guitar or even tormented his little sister, Becky? What about constantly seeing his back searching through the fridge for something to eat, telling me "Dude I'm starved," to which I would always laugh and say, "But we just had dinner!" He was my bottomless pit, and it seemed that I could never keep enough milk in the house.

How would I be able to tell Melissa and Becky their brother wouldn't be coming back home? How would we ever manage without his pranks? There would be a terrible void. A cold chill ran down my spine and again I cried out, "Please don't take my son from me!"

As the hours of searching continued, the waves wouldn't cease their angry thrashings on the shore; there was still no sight of Jaren or his surfboard. Each time I tried to find hope in the absence of his surfboard, common sense thundered through my mind that there was no way Jaren could survive such a storm as this. How could *anyone* survive such a storm?

The Coast Guard ship had searched up and down the coast with no sign of Jaren or his surfboard bobbing in the erratic and choppy waves. When they were satisfied they had done all they could do, they headed back to the safety of the harbor. I don't remember being notified that they had left. Looking back, telling me would have been like telling me there was absolutely no hope. I'm sure the Sheriff didn't want me to know that the Coast Guard crew was no longer searching for my boy.

Jaren was officially out there on his own and the hours were ticking on. I continued to pray that he was still holding on to his surfboard. I knew it would be his only resource to help him stay above water. He must be exhausted and hungry. What could possibly be going through his mind out there all by himself in that storm? Was he afraid? Was hyperthermia setting in by now? *Hang on Jaren*, I cried to myself.

Chapter Fifteen

Back to Where the Whole Ordeal Began

J aren remembers:

Eventually, I managed to paddle nearly all the way back to Faria where this whole ordeal had begun. I was feeling very depleted from the hours of paddling in the frigid ocean. The situation began to feel dire again as I realized I was having trouble paddling effectively. Instead of oars driving through the water, my arms felt like wet noodles. If I were to make it past Faria to the bay where I thought I had the best chance to get through the giant surf, I had to paddle more.

I was low on energy and very weak. I was experiencing the early stages of hypothermia. I began to think about how hungry I was. At one point I focused my attention on the Faria campground store and thought about the delicious burgers I often ate there after a surf.

Suddenly I saw a bright light some ways off in the ocean to the south towards Ventura. It was getting closer. It was a thick beam of light shooting in all sorts of directions with no particular pattern. As it drew closer, I realized it was the searchlight of a Coast Guard vessel looking for me. A huge sense of relief came over me. I was going to be plucked out of the cold sea and this predicament I found myself in would be over. I began to hoot and holler trying to get the attention of the vessel. Realizing it would be difficult to spot me in my black wetsuit at night, I got off my surfboard and began treading water holding my white surfboard over my head hoping that it would be easier to spot.

It was clear that they had no clue where to look for me as their search route was very broad. The boat came very near to my location several times and would then change course and motor away off into the distance almost disappearing completely at times. Every time the boat came back, I had new hope that they would see or hear me that time. Although the bright light would shine directly at me, my black wet suit and white surfboard blended in with the choppy waves, and the vessel disappeared one more time and then finally never came back.

That was my lowest point. I was alone again. I had burned precious energy screaming and waving my surfboard around trying to get the attention of the boat. I was so tired I could hardly stay awake. I remember laying on my surfboard resting my head on the deck and nodding off only to be awakened by water splashing in my face. I had woken up three times vomiting under water.

It was then clear to me that if I didn't paddle myself into shore, I wouldn't make it through the night.

Chapter Sixteen

Please Don't Take My Son

T he anxiety of not knowing where or how to find Jaren was para-
lyzing. It seemed like only yesterday when I held him in my arms
for the very first time. He had arrived at 8 pounds, 5 ounces. I counted
all his little toes and fingers and gently stroked his soft golden hair. He
was perfect! I clearly remember thanking God for our beautiful little baby
boy and promising Him that I would take good care of Jaren and watch
after him, just as I had promised a little over two years earlier when I gave
birth to our sweet Melissa. Less than two years after that, I would once
again make these same promises after giving birth to our precious little
Rebecca.

With each birth, I made huge promises to God that I would take care
of each one of my babies. It was so easy back then. I could kiss their little
boo boos and hold them in my arms if ever they were afraid. I always
had super hero bandages a-plenty for even the smallest of owies. Now,

my little ones were growing into young adults and their needs were ever changing. Still, I never forgot the promises I had made to God. I felt like I had failed to live up to those promises tonight when I could not find my son.

Jaren's welfare was completely out of my control and the guilt was excruciating. I felt like I was failing my son. Were there any warnings about this event I had not paid attention to? Was I so wrapped up in my own world not to see what was coming? How could I have known he would venture out in this storm? Did my mother's intuition fail me?

I continued to pray that he would be protected by the unseen powers and grace of God. I hoped the winds would cease and allow the helicopter search team to join with the Coast Guard crew. Now neither were in pursuit of Jaren's whereabouts. The rain had finally lightened a bit, but the wind shears were still too dangerous for a helicopter. It was now reported to be grounded indefinitely.

Any feelings of hope I tried to muster were only met with stronger feelings of despair. Everything was stacking up against a happy ending at this point of the night. The hours crept on. There was still a dim glimmer of hope since no surfboard had washed up on shore. Even so, I couldn't help from crashing down into lower and lower depths of grief while looking out into the dark, menacing froth. From where I stood on the rocky shore, I couldn't even see past the breakwater. Still, I was frozen to the spot and refused to relinquish my watchpoint.

The ocean showed no signs of mercy for my son. It seemed to delight at my inability to see any sign of him. Everything was in turmoil, and the negative voices inside me clamored even louder for center stage with the brutal words that I would never see my son again. These voices continued to challenge me in my struggle to cling to any amount of faith and hope that the divine powers of God could and would be there for Jaren.

The night continued advancing with the haunting reality of still no sight or sign of Jaren. By now, he could be miles out to sea in any direction. The storm was in charge of his whereabouts. I pleaded with God to hold him close in the safety of His arms. I pleaded for Jaren to have the ability to keep his mind alert and use his strength where it would be needed most. Knowing exactly where and how to search for him was impossible from the shore.

Cruel torment continued its bombardment of voices against me as I struggled to hold on to any amount of faith or hope. Each principle that could only contradict the reality of what was really playing out before my own eyes was under attack, and I was feeling more out of touch with my own thoughts.

I was taught from a very young age that faith is a hope of things not seen but hoped for and believed. At that hour, could I honestly believe this principal that I had grown up with? As difficult and unrealistic as it seemed, there continued to be the unwavering still, small voice in my mind telling me, yes, I could believe. This still, small voice would wage against all the other shouts in my mind and was a powerful spark of my inner peace. Though so very fleeting at times, it continued to be my anchor in the storm. It gave me the courage to hold on to the promising words of Bishop Martin spoken so many hours earlier.

I kept these feelings to myself. It was already apparent to many around me that I was crumbling under the severity of the situation. I was sure sharing my feelings of such peace would only make me look more unstable, so I continued straining my eyes, trying to take in as much of the ocean's breadth as I could.

My once beloved ocean had become my enemy. How would I ever be able to look at her again, knowing she had viciously taken my son from me? If that was the case, I swore I would despise the ocean for the rest of my life. And what if his broken body were to be found somewhere mangled on the rocky shoreline? I yelled out to the ocean as loud as I could, "PLEASE! DON'T TAKE MY SON FROM ME!"

Chapter Seventeen

How Could I Claim His Lifeless Body?

U nder the billowing, raging sky, every hopeless thought and fear began to torture my mother heart in greater force. How would I be able to claim his lifeless body or worse yet, what if he were never found, only to be buried beneath the sea in a place I would never know of? The horrifying reality of sharks in the ocean continued streaking through my mind. As the myriad of horrible thoughts filled every space in my mind, I found it harder to fight.

Truly my faith and hope were more like a tiny mustard seed while trying to believe the promising words of Bishop Martin, "Your son's going to be okay." I knew deep down that my faltering faith wouldn't dictate Jaren's outcome. Even still, I didn't want to give in to my doubts regardless of my hesitancy to truly believe. "Dear Father above!" I cried out in defiance at the angry shouts in my mind. "Please keep the sharks away from my son!"

Finding another place alone near the water's edge, my weary eyes strained even harder to capture any glimpse of Jaren. Still there was no indication of a calming of the sea or sight of Jaren to be found.

As hope seemed to ebb and flow with the crashing of the waves, my faith would again give way to doubt and fear. I remember seeing groups in the shadows slowly making their way back to their cars. My heart sank. I was torn between wanting to be alone and needing a community of supporters and hoping everyone would stay. Their presence seemed like an affirmation of hope. And their leaving seemed to confirm the hopelessness of the situation. *Please don't leave*, my heart cried out!

I found myself arguing with God in anguished sobs, exclaiming that I believed with all my heart that God knew exactly where Jaren was. My pleadings would not cease. I was frantically praying for a miracle. Over and over, I exclaimed to the Heavens as if to counsel them about how miracles can and do happen. It was as if I were trying to summon the very powers of Heaven to answer my pleas.

Of course, deep down inside, I knew that God had all the power and that He is over all things. But surely taking my son at such a young age couldn't be in this plan. NO! I recoiled at such a thought! It just couldn't happen this way!

These haunting thoughts shouted out against all my hope and faith while my mind was pulled into the darkest gloom. I revisited his whole life as it flashed before my eyes. "My Buck-A-Roo can't really be gone!" I screamed back at the menacing voices in my mind.

My Buck-A-Roo! A nickname we gave him when he was about three years old. We had been to Santa Barbara Pier that day. The same day he asked about the wide pipe leading into the harbor and if it was the hose Heavenly Father used to fill the ocean. Later that night, when he was saying his prayers, and in that cute little lisp of his, he exclaimed, "Thanks for the nice day, Buck-A-Roo!" Doug and I had a hard time keeping a straight face.

Now thirteen years later, my little Buck-A-Roo was lost in that same ocean. Bursting into tears and then needing to pull myself back together again was a constant tug-of-war. I struggled with the ability to keep my emotions from dismissing any sense of rational thinking. I needed to stay calm. Completely falling apart wasn't an option. This wasn't about my feelings. It was about finding him!

As the hours of uncertainty and fear continued, so did the onslaught of voices and inner battles in the chambers of my mind. The voices were becoming much more chaotic than all the noise of the storm, proving to create an intensity of a great mental storm within my own soul.

In all attempts to find my son, my anguish and fear grew even stronger. But I still pleaded and tried to reason with the Heavens, to please spare my son. Still no sight of Jaren was found.

What about the fears and danger he was facing out there all alone? Was he praying there while the many on shore and at home were also praying with him? Would he be able to sense that many were praying for his safety? Were angels with him, helping him stay on his board? Were there others there who had already passed from this life, helping him in all possible ways? There had to be!

In my struggle, I began feeling a strong sense that Jaren had a purpose in surviving. These feelings were bright against the dark backdrop of uncertainty. I continued to fight hard to grasp tightly to my own faith and hope.

I tried to somehow communicate in spirit to Jaren to not give up and to hold onto his board. I wanted him to feel and know that we were there looking for him. Surely this may sound crazy to some. But for a desperate mother, I didn't care what anyone would think or should think of me, and I still don't. My renewed energy was focusing on a more spiritual level of ability, if possible, to help Jaren be aware that I was there for him. For that matter, I wanted him to know we were all desperately there for him. I was willing to exert anything and everything possible. I fought to believe it was possible for him to feel my reaching out to him.

Chapter Eighteen

Peace Against the Turmoil and Others By His Side

In the midst of all the searching, shouting, crashing and storming around me, I couldn't ignore the peace that lingered in my mind. As uncertain as I was of the outcome, I still believed that God knew where Jaren was. I was fighting a true battle of spiritual yearnings over common sense, trying to believe that God was aware of how hard I was trying to hold on to my faith and hope. I was hoping he would reward my faith and assure me that Jaren was still alive and would survive. Jaren needed a miracle and only God could make that happen.

As the hours crawled slowly by and the storm raged on, something changed. Though unrecognizable at first, I began to feel something different about this storm. I began to feel the sense of being in the eye of a hurricane. All seemed to hush and stand still around me while the outside whirlwind of chaos churned more fiercely. I suddenly wasn't feeling threatened. I felt as though I were in a safe place, observing the screaming wind and the mountainous waves through a thin veil. All actions and noises became distorted in a sort of melting kind of way. I felt a growing sense of calm within me and was beginning to truly feel at peace. My frantic mind tried hard to pierce the veil to make me believe I just might be losing my mind after all.

I was afraid to share my feelings with those around me. I felt like they would think I had completely lost it by now. The demonizing thoughts wouldn't cease. I would be told days later that some of my friends and family thought I was beginning to shut down emotionally because my words and actions were becoming more isolated as the hours dragged on with no sign of our missing boy or his board and all hopes grew increasingly grim. I had, to them, become inexplicably distant and calm in my actions.

All these years later, I am still unable to express how I was able to have those feelings of calm when I knew Jaren was no match for that storm or the fury of the ocean. I had to trust in the omniscient power of God that night. Choosing to trust made all the difference.

To be able to say that my feelings in the midst of an unimaginable tragedy were tempered by moments of spiritual enlightenment would be an understatement. Though I may not have realized it at the time, there was a very thin veil between my mortal reality and my spiritual existence. I was stretched beyond my natural ability to trust, hope, breathe, believe and at the same time know! My faith was becoming a vivid truth. My son must certainly survive!

I had a distinct feeling that, in addition to my grandmother, there were others by my side, unseen by the human eye. I had the strong sense that my Ashton grandparents were there and also Jaren's Coler great-grandparents. I genuinely felt the presence of loved ones who had long passed away.

I didn't dare share this with the others during our search. But I had the undeniable feeling that Jaren wasn't out there fighting to survive all by himself. All these years later, I still know this is true when I tell others of that night.

Some may just pass me off as being overly religious or spiritual or for that matter just plain delusional! But I know what I felt, and I cannot deny what I felt and experienced that night.

To say I was holding on to my faith doesn't mean I indulged in wishful thinking. I believe that deep assurance within me was real. I certainly don't want to seem like a fairytale girl who believed everything always had a "happily ever after" ending. This wasn't the case. I'm not that girl. Rather, it was a distinctive and factual feeling I had deep down inside. I wasn't about to push it aside no matter the hopelessness of the situation. I believed in a higher power. I needed to believe.

A strange energy was beginning to create a different feeling in the atmosphere around me. The unexplainable feeling was becoming stronger than I could even try to comprehend. There seemed to be a new, unseeable light kindled in the darkness. Was Jaren feeling the same changes of the atmospheric energies that I was feeling? It felt as though the Heavens may be reaching out. But how many of us recognized the shift in the energy that was taking place?

Faith was a rollercoaster struggle as the hours pressed on. Yet, deep within me was that spirit of assurance whispering in my ears that my son would be okay just as Bishop Martin had said to me. Even through the loud roar of wind and rain, I was still somehow able to hear that still, small voice reassuring me. I believe I wasn't alone and somehow knew Jaren wasn't alone either. There were unseen forces working together on his behalf.

***

In his words:

After many hours of paddling, stopping only for brief rests, the wind died down and the sky cleared up. I felt a sense of peace for the first time and I became more aware of my immediate surroundings. I began noticing there was quite a bit of sea life around me. I became aware of dorsal fins slicing through the surface of the waves. My first thought was, sharks! Any pretense of bravery was gone and I quickly pulled my feet and hands out of the water on top of my surfboard. Sharks were the last thing I needed stalking me out in the open water while I was doing everything I could just to hang on in the dark waves. Relief washed over me when I realized they were dolphins. They seemed to be circling me and my board. I felt somewhat protected by them and was glad they were there with me.

At times, there were gulls and other sea birds sitting on the water near me. I felt some kind of connection to these animals. In a way they offered some sort of company, which felt nice.

I also noticed there were lines of neon blue streaking through the water all around and underneath me. I later understood that the blue glow was caused by an algae bloom commonly referred to as "Red Tide." Red Tide is caused by a chemical reaction that results from the movement of the algae. Fish moving through the water cause the algae to glow. At times, I saw very large streaks of blue which left me wondering what kind of fish were in the vicinity...

***

I just knew my boy wasn't alone out there on the storm tossed sea. Let people think what they will, but I had no thought of caring what others might think of me. All that mattered to me was doing everything in my power to act with faith and hope while my eyes and heart continued to attempt to pierce through the storm in an effort to find a glimpse of Jaren. I wanted silence from all noises around me in hopes of hearing his voice above the sounds of the waves still hurling violently to shore. The storm seemed to die down a bit and the rain had stopped. But the wind and the ocean were still of a very angry disposition.

In those languishing hours I wouldn't be able to fully recognize the orchestrated events taking place on shore and at sea where Jaren was, even as I felt the energies around me shift. I wasn't able to see what Jaren might be doing in his own struggle to be found. I would not stop consciously trying to communicate the encouragement of my soul for him not to give up!

I became acutely aware of how tired Jaren must have been by that time. All of us on shore were drenched, windblown and fatigued. Determination mixed with adrenaline was the only thing keeping us alert.

My mind and body began to play games, taking over in slow motion. Everyone was on autopilot as the hours passed without any sign of Jaren. No one wanted to give up. Not even the countless kind strangers who continued to search alongside us. Many had never heard his name before the news broke of a missing surfer off the Ventura Coast. Finding Jaren was our united purpose. In those hours, we all came together to search for this missing sixteen-year-old boy lost at sea.

As time wore on, people began to give up and quietly stepped away from view, returning to their homes not knowing what Jaren's fate would be. Surely these good people watched and listened to the next morning's news with baited breath, waiting to learn of Jaren's fate.

Like everyone else, I was soaked to the bone, standing in the blowing wind and rain in wet, sand filled shoes. I was numb to the elements of the storm, even though shivers convulsed in my body as I tried to picture where my son could possibly be out there in that angry ocean.

Still, the flood lights from the coastal beach homes and searchlights of the rescue parties beamed on brightly into the dark, churning ocean.

Darkness and light. Such polarizing opposites. It was a night filled with the extremes of both. I could understand why people began to leave. They saw no hope in the darkness. However, those who still held out hope were for me a huge beacon of light in those ensuing hours. I wanted the growing light inside of me to shine bright enough for them to be buoyed by it as well as we continued holding out hope when all seemed hopeless.

Chapter Nineteen

Still No Sign of Jaren

I yearned to turn back the years to when I held my baby boy for the first time in my arms. I was again reflecting on the first time I held his precious little body close to mine.

"He is now in your arms," I prayed to God. *"Please keep him safe. Don't let him fall off his board. If he does, help him get right back on."* Staying afloat on his surfboard seemed to be his only hope.

The worry of a mother can never be expressed in words. The shock of the event cut deep in my heart as my anguish intensified, wondering where he could possibly be.

I continued to wander up and down the beach on my own in my isolation of thought and prayer. I was still surrounded by people who hadn't given up and gone home. Many I didn't even know still combed the coastline looking for any sign of Jaren. I had feelings of comfort knowing so many were still there. We were all there to find Jaren. People I would never know or be able to thank were like angels to me, doing their part to bring Jaren back to safety.

Time was moving slower and slower. This was alarming as my mind raced even faster. The horrible "what ifs" swirled through my head with blistering intensity. Fighting to keep my head level was frightening. There were too many voices shouting in my head. These voices wanted me to believe there was no hope for my son! They wanted me to know I was a fool to believe he could survive!

I wanted to hold God accountable to my faith. Yet I knew deep inside it's not for me to dictate His will. In no way would I want to sound disrespectful of Deity. But I knew God knew where Jaren was and my prayers wouldn't cease in praying and acknowledging He could and would bring Jaren safely back to shore. Surely my God of Miracles would do this! Right? Oh how much I wanted this to also be God's will!

Still trying to communicate in spirit with Jaren, I wanted him to be reassured that we were all at the shorelines looking for him. I wanted him to hold onto his board and not give up. I wanted him to trust that God could safely bring him back.

Through all the commotion of sounds of people, wind, and the crashing waves, it was as if almost everything was moving in slow and muted motion. The voices in my mind competed to be heard more than the others. Voices of reason. Voices of faith. Yet the loudest voice of all – despair.

Once again at the command post, Doug and I were speaking with some of the rescue team. It was obvious they were carefully trying to prepare us for the worst-case scenario. However, we could not accept the worst-case scenario. Not our son! Words were muffled with confusion and disbelief as we grappled with the fact that he had been lost for almost ten hours. He was last seen waving his hands above his head screaming for help as the strong current of the riptide pulled him further out to sea.

Pulling myself together and clinging tightly to the words "your son's going to be okay." I reached deep inside for the strength to hold up strong and believe.

If the worst happened, I would never be able to look out at the ocean's majestic beauty ever again. To even hear the sounds of the waves only tormented my aching soul. How could I have not been able to prevent such a terrible event from happening?

I felt guilty for encouraging him to surf. When he was only thirteen, I would watch from the beach, jumping up and down with excitement at each wave he so effortlessly caught. I've always been the kind of proud mom not embarrassed at all to yell out for all to hear "HEY! THAT'S MY SON!!"

I bought him his new/used wetsuit barely two months earlier and couldn't wait until his birthday to give it to him. Now, I was standing on the beaten and rain-soaked shore of the beach, defeated at the thought of losing him. I wished I had never encouraged him to surf.

By now, it was past midnight. More people were leaving the beach. They left thinking their search had been in vain. This was a depressing scene of sorrowing friends and strangers slowly making their way out of sight.

Doug and I had been in and out of the mobile command post all this time. We had just traveled up by Pitas Point where Jaren and his friends had jumped the wall to the beach so many hours earlier. We had been in close communication with the search party throughout the night, now approaching the early hours of the next day.

We discussed any possible options we could take moving forward. They weren't good options, like waiting for the break of day to resume the search or until conditions improved so that they could send out the coast guard ship or the helicopter. But the winds continued to howl, preventing the rescue team from doing all they wanted to do.

Looking back, words cannot express my gratitude for all whose efforts were put forth so bravely in searching for my son. Including all the people who, upon hearing the news on TV or radio, dropped what they were doing and came rushing to the shores up and down Ventura County coastline that night to help with our search. During those hours, strangers became united in one cause – finding and rescuing my son! My heart will always be gratefully filled for each who came that night.

My son wasn't a baby in my arms anymore. So quickly growing up, he was now sixteen years old. I couldn't just reach out to gather him in my arms or make any hurt or fear go away. He was out of my reach and that had to be the most terrorizing experience I believe any mother can go through.

I was also aware that a different sense of guilt had found its way as I prayed for his welfare. I was experiencing what other mothers had felt as they had pleaded for the safe return or miraculous rescues or healings of their loved ones. Why should my prayer be any different than the prayers of those whose stories didn't have a "happy ending?" Guilt and other emotions were constantly at war one with another intruding in on every sense and feeling I was living and breathing during those tumultuous hours. Yet, the resounding words of my Bishop would again be the resounding echo in my mind, "Your son's going to be okay." So soft and clear were these words, so very hard to hear over all the clatter of my mind, I wanted to believe.

The anguish of my feelings that night are with me even as I am now writing. The terror and the hope, and the unmistakable conviction that I felt that Jaren had not fulfilled his purpose on the earth. I didn't care what that purpose might be. My only care was that he be found alive!

Chapter Twenty

Jaren is Alive!

J aren made a final effort:

I began paddling directly towards shore. I was just off the top of Faria point. I didn't have enough energy left to paddle down the point to the bay where the waves would be more forgiving. I was going to have to paddle in right at the top of the point. As I slowly edged my way closer to where the waves were breaking, I suddenly felt scared and nervous again. I could hear the rumbling of the surf. I could tell by the deep thundering sound of the waves breaking just inside of where I was that they were large and powerful.

Slowly, I made my way closer to the breaking waves. I was starting to feel the rise and fall of large swells rolling underneath me. I could hear the explosion of waves detonating on the water. I couldn't see much but all my other senses were screaming danger. I reached a point where I felt I was just out past the breaking waves and sat on my board for a few minutes trying to muster up the courage to make a paddle for shore.

The waves were now lifting me and getting very steep. I could see the tops of the waves feathering as the breeze raced up their faces right before they broke. I understood I was now far enough in that a large set of waves could break behind me and smother me. This was my big fear.

I was waiting for a lull in the waves to time my passage through the impact zone. I layed back down on my board and began paddling in. It was scary not being able to see what was coming at me. I knew the waves were big but couldn't see them coming until they were almost right on top of me.

The only way to detect a wave coming was to monitor the rise and fall of the horizon. When a wave was approaching the horizon seemed to lift. The low lying stars on the horizon would disappear as the walls of black water rose towards me.

I was paddling with the little strength I had left when I crossed the point of no return. I was now approaching the impact zone, the area in which waves were consistently breaking. I remember looking over my shoulder and seeing a giant wall of black. This one wasn't going to roll underneath me. This one was going to break right on me. I knew that my surfboard was my life-saving flotation device at that point, and I wasn't going to let it out of my grasp no matter what. I wrapped my arms around my surfboard as tight as I could and wasn't gonna let go. The wave broke almost right on top of me.

I was suddenly being violently tossed and turned under water. I recall feeling the rocks on the bottom a few times which was scary because I was down pretty deep. All I could do was hold on to my surfboard and ride it out. Eventually, I surfaced only to be battered by a few more crashing waves.

Eventually I was washed far enough in that I could stand up. I couldn't believe it. I was on shore. I made it! I picked my board up out of the water and noticed it had a crease right through the middle of it. The initial impact of the first wave had nearly pushed my body right through my surfboard. It was incredible how much energy I suddenly had considering how depleted I was minutes ago. I ran right across the jagged rocks towards the sea wall and the homes on the point.

I was able to jump over a residence's fence and ran through their property towards the front gate of the community where I knew there was a payphone. I needed to check in with my dad because he was probably wondering where I was. This is when I realized how long I was actually out in the ocean. I made a collect call to my house. My sister, Melissa, answered the phone with a somber voice. I said "It's Jaren, where's Dad?" She replied in a hysterical tone, "Where are you!?" I told her I was at Faria. "It's 2:30 in the morning and everyone is looking for you!" she screamed.

***

Melissa and Becky had been home waiting for any word. They were losing hope as the night turned to the early hours of the next day. The phone rang, and with fear of what this phone call could mean, she somberly answered. But the voice she heard shook her to the very core: Jaren's voice. She couldn't believe her ears and she explained everything that had taken place while he had been lost at sea. She contacted the police, who agreed that a miracle had truly happened! Our Jaren was ALIVE!

***

Crowded in the command post discussing our next efforts, I heard a call come in. There was a sudden look of shock on the Sheriff's face and in his voice. He turned to us and exclaimed that Jaren had been found and was alive!

Doug and I scrambled into the backseat of a patrol car. We had left the very same area just before Jaren was washed back to shore. We had been there minutes earlier and now moved back down closer to Ventura. We had no idea of the length and width of the coastline Jaren had been dragged around during those frightful hours at sea.

I remember a voice on the CB radio telling the patrol car sheriff to "kick his butt" when you see him. I chimed in, "That's my son you're talking about!" The voice on the other end then went silent as we drove on. We had gone from the lowest of lows to the highest of highs within a matter of minutes, and our hearts raced faster than the car could drive. *Could this really be happening? Is he really alive? What just happened?!*

Within a few short minutes, we found where Jaren had made the call. The headlights of the patrol car shone on him lying at the side of the road on his surfboard.

As Doug and I sprang out of the car, Jaren wasn't moving. Our hearts stopped until we realized he had fallen asleep waiting for help. We breathed a collective sigh of relief. As we helped him back to his feet, I could see his lips were blue. With a trembling voice and shivering fits, he spoke the words, "Dude, I'm starved." My heart leaped, and I can never express my joy as he spoke those words! I knew then without any doubt that my Buck-A-Roo was truly going to be okay!

Joyfully returning to the command post, we were greeted with an anxious and somewhat disbelieving crew waiting to take his vitals to make sure he was indeed okay. There was not one of us there who wasn't experiencing the highest of highs or complete shock! We were all witnessing a miracle! Especially Jaren. He had overcome all the elements that fought to take him away from us. He was able to overcome, survive, and navigate all the obstacles against him during those long dark hours in the turbulent storm. And this, because of a God of Miracles who watched over and protected him against all the odds!

Jaren couldn't have known that when he first pointed his surfboard towards the waves early that afternoon before, he would find himself fighting to stay alive throughout the night and early hours. He would fight fear, fatigue, hyperthermia, hunger and the most powerful of all, the storm until finally he was caught in a that miraculous wave as it came crashing down upon him and washed him safely to shore. This truly was a majestic witness of God's greatness!

How can I adequately express my gratitude? How can I even begin to understand the magnitude of all the events of that night?

Though Jaren would later recall what he went through all those hours, I still get emotional when I recount the events of that night. Hearing his words and how his ordeal at sea, along with ours on shore, were so intermingling is a witness of the reality of God's love and mercy. I continue to be in awe at what his words would later express.

***

He said about the final events of that night:

I don't remember anything after that. I must have passed out or went to sleep for some reason right there on the highway because the next thing I remember was my parents waking me up. They helped me up off the pavement and we got in a police car. We were taken to a mobile command center set up by the police a few miles down the road. They wanted to evaluate me and make sure I didn't need to go to the hospital. I got out of my wetsuit, and they gave me some blankets to warm me up. I was absolutely starving at that point. It was odd that the only thing they had for me to eat was a small box of raisins. The authorities decided I was only slightly hypothermic and just needed food and sleep. I recall driving back to my Dad's house with Mom and Aunt Cindy in her family's suburban.

I didn't want this to be a big deal. I knew I scared my friends and family half to death, but I just wanted everything to be normal again. So, I went to school the next morning.

I was shocked at the reactions my schoolmates had upon seeing me. I didn't realize that most of those kids had gone to bed without knowing that I ever came in. I was presumed dead by most. I was like a ghost walking around campus.

***

Yes! Truly a great miracle had taken place! I learned that the matchless power of God cannot be thwarted by the laws of nature. I learned that God truly does know our hearts' desires and answers our prayers. I came away from this experience with a greater respect that His will doesn't always reflect ours and that there is a much greater amount of understanding we must all come to when our prayers aren't answered. Are we able to truly see His will even in those moments of great loss or sorrow? Can we recognize the true miracle that God is in the details and that one day all tears will be wiped away? How willing are we *really* to choose faith over fear when the world comes crashing in around us?

Are we able to recognize God's gracious love for each of us? Though we cannot now fully understand why there is so much pain and suffering, one day we will all see him face to face, and all things will be made manifest, and finally we will look back on our lives and see how He safely guided us home. Some are called home sooner, and we can't understand why. We think it cruel, and, yes, there is so much that is cruel and hard to understand. But I believe God takes no one home until they have finished their purpose in this life. I also believe He waits with open arms and the promises of a future reunion for all loved ones.

I thank God everyday for the matchless miracle of not allowing that terrible storm in all her fury to take Jaren away from us that night. I also look back and realize that unknowingly I did pay attention to the warning signs of this night's impending danger. It was the strong impression I kept getting the day I bought Jaren's wetsuit. Had I not heeded those impressions of Jaren needing to have the more expensive and thickest wetsuit, hypothermia would have seized upon him much earlier, and he wouldn't have been able survive those long hours in the cold, forbidding waves. Years later, it would become clear to me that I did heed this very strong impression, not knowing this was a voice of warning two months earlier. I had not failed Jaren as I thought I did during those awful hours of guilt and fear while searching for him at the water's edge. I came away knowing that Jaren has yet to finish the purposes God has in store for his life as He does for each of us.

May we each look to God in all things. May we pay attention to the valuable impressions and promptings we may be given and put our trust in Him, even when the voices of doubt and fear try to distract us from His gentle guidance, love, wisdom and above all, all that He has in store for us.

All are children of God. All are valuable! We cannot fully comprehend all His ways and dealings with our own lives as He does. But if we can put our trust in Him, one day all things will be made known, and we will praise Him for His compassion, wisdom and unfailing love. His unfathomable love for everyone who ever lived before, now and hereafter. He created the heavens and the earth. He created all things, and we are all His children and His crowning joy!

***

Today, as I look out upon the ocean, I am filled with a renewed reverence for her majesty and might. Never again will I take for granted her power and magnitude, as I did so many years ago, standing on the planks of a well worn pier, feeling the splashes of her waves burst through, defying the bounds of man. I used to believe that the ocean was the mistress of her many moods and capricious nature. After spending such a turbulent, tumultuous night by her side, I now understand that even she, in all her fury, is subject to the God in Heaven who is a God of miracles. He is over all and is mindful of each of us throughout our every storm and trial, come what may. For if God were not a God of miracles, this story would have never been written.

Big Wednesday
December 13, 1995
Ventura, California
Veronica Phin

STORM CAUSES HEAVY DAMAGE

TEEN FOUND ALIVE

COMPLETE COVERAGE INSIDE

*For I am God,
and mine arm is not shortened,
and I will show miracles,
signs and wonders,
unto all those
who believe on my name.*

D&C 35:8

"These are very dangerous conditions. Even the experts can get wiped out by this stuff."

— Rob Krohn
Oxnard Weather Service

Surfer Survives 10 Chilling Hours at Sea

By KENNETH R. WEISS
Times Staff Writer

VENTURA—Slipping off his surfboard, Jaren Coler awakened choking on seawater. His body erupted in spasms of coughing and then he vomited.

It was the blind time he had thrown up. He was getting colder by the hour, starting to drift in and out of consciousness.

The shivering 16-year-old surfer from Camarillo recognized the signs of hypothermia.

"I didn't think I was going to die until I started to fall asleep," Jaren said. Wednesday, sitting in the kitchen of his Camarillo home, the teenage surfer recounted how a quick after-school surf outing turned into a 10-hour ordeal during Tuesday night's storm—with Jaren bobbing helplessly beyond the breakers off Pirat Point north of Ventura.

He could see the flashlight beams of crews searching the rock-strewn shoreline off Faria Beach.

As first, he couldn't paddle in, defeated by rip currents that swept him far out to sea. Later, he decided to wait for the monstrous surf would calm so he could make a successful landing on the rocky shoreline.

But waves of fear began to wash over him when a Coast Guard boat disappeared. It had come within 200 feet on several occasions and sent its shore a spotlight on his face.

"I decided if I was going to die, I should die trying to get in.

Please see SURFER, B3

Jaren Coler

ALAN HAGMAN / Los Angeles Times

This newspaper collage was given to Cheri Kane by a dear friend, Lori Merrill-Kao

Cowabunga! Stamina, luck save Camarillo teen

He survives 10-hour ordeal at sea on surfboard

By Rick Nielsen
Staff writer

Staff photo by **Victoria Sayer Pearson**

> **"I** thought I was going to die. I took a beating, but I finally managed to fight through the pounding waves and hang onto my surfboard until I was washed to shore."
>
> **—Jaren Coler**

A 16-year-old surfer credited stamina and luck for surviving a nearly 10-hour ordeal of being thrashed by a treacherous, storm-churned sea off Faria Beach.

"I thought I was going to die," said Jaren Coler, a Camarillo High School junior. "I took a beating, but I finally managed to fight through the pounding waves and hang onto my surfboard until I was washed to shore."

Standing in front of his Camarillo home Wednesday, Coler displayed his cracked surfboard as evidence of his harrowing experience that began about 5 p.m. Tuesday and ended about 2:30 a.m. Wednesday. He vowed to never surf during a storm again.

"No way!" said the 5-foot-9, 150-pound teen whom friends describe as very athletic. "I don't want to die."

Steve White, supervising lifeguard for the Buenaventura State Beach, said the surf has been terrible.

"It is very dangerous and will beat up a body badly," he said Wednesday. "It's not good for surfing."

Coler's problems began when he became separated from his friend while riding waves at Faria Beach, a popular surfing spot along the Rincon northwest of Ventura.

"The waves were so big and rough I couldn't get to shore. I just laid on my board until the surf got smaller," Coler said. "The waves instead got bigger and bigger. I knew I was in trouble."

When he couldn't find his friend, Chris Cohea, 17, of Camarillo ran to a nearby house and called authorities to report Coler missing.

Within two hours, 30 rescue workers from the Ventura County Sheriff's Department and the Coast Guard Station at Channel Islands Harbor were searching the beach and ocean. They were joined by Coler's family and friends. The massive search ended at 2:30 a.m. when Coler managed to paddle through the churning surf and called home.

The conversation reportedly went like this: " 'Where's dad?' " Coler asked his sister, Becky 14.

Please see **SURFER** *on* **A8**

SURFER: Teen survives sea ordeal

Continued from **A1**

" 'Where are you?' " she said excitedly. " 'Everybody is looking for you.' "

Becky said she called the command post and told her father, Douglas Coler, her brother had made it to the beach.

Douglas Coler said he rushed to his son from the command post, which was less than a minute away.

"He was exhausted, hungry and extremely cold, but after feeding and warming him he was just fine," Douglas Coler said. "I was worried. But I had the feeling that Jaren would either be found or would make it to shore himself because his board was not discovered on shore."

"I got really cold and very sick while being knocked around by the current," young Coler said. "It was scary."

At one point, he said, he saw a U.S. Coast Guard rescue boat.

"It was about 200 feet away. I yelled as loud as I could and put my board up high to get their attention but they apparently did not see me," Jaren said.

Ventura County Star, December 14, 1995. Article by Rick Nielsen. Photo by Victoria Sayer Pearson.

Ventura County Star, December 14, 1995. Article by Richard Warchol. Image by Gary Phelps of Aspen Helicopters. Article continued on next page.

This image details the extensive destruction of the historic Ventura wooden pier. Up until that night, this was the longest pier in North and South America. As noted in the story, Jaren's friends had ventured out to the end of the pier in hopes of spotting Jaren in the waves. Had these friends not fled when they heard the cracking beneath their feet, they would have most likely lost their lives.

What happened

Strong westerly winds from Tuesday's storm whipped down the coast, causing unobstructed swells which hit the end of the Ventura pier with full force. About 420 feet of the pier completely washed out.

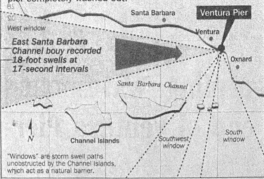

West window

East Santa Barbara Channel bouy recorded 18-foot swells at 17-second intervals

Santa Barbara

Ventura Pier

Ventura

Oxnard

Santa Barbara Channel

N

Channel Islands

Southwest window

South window

"Windows" are storm swell paths unobstructed by the Channel Islands, which act as a natural barrier.

Source: City of San Buenaventura

Staff graphic by **Wendy Noda**

PIER: Shut down again by storm

Continued from **A1**

cost or how long it takes, the city should rebuild.

"It's a landmark," said Ken Faulks of Ventura. "I'd like to see them do it again. But it needs to be done right."

"I think it's worth it," said Pierpont Beach resident Leo West. "It brings so much tourism and business. It's a shame."

Built in 1872, the 1,958-foot pier has had a rough time of it since being destroyed during heavy winter storms in 1986 when 12-foot breakers battered it and knocked out four piles. Storms swept away another 35 piles in the following weeks. It reopened in 1993 after a $3.5 million renovation. Just 15 months later, fierce storms hit again, knocking out 60 piles and jarring loose 30 others. The pier reopened again 10 months ago after $500,000 in repairs.

"It's a tough place to have a pier" because of its direct-line exposure to western swells, said Lee Cushman, part owner of the Santa Barbara-based Cushman Contracting Corp., the company that did the construction work. "It's like putting a dang heater in the middle of Antarctica. You're trying to fight Mother Nature in an awkward spot."

Officials at the Long Beach-based Moffatt and Nichol Engineers, the firm that designed the pier renovation, were not available for comment Wednesday.

Meanwhile, state officials closed San Buenaventura State Beach from the pier southwest to Marina Park while pier debris is cleaned up. Some of the piles appeared snapped in two, with their often rusted, 12-inch iron bolts bent and sticking out.

"Twisted like pretzels," said Norman Elton, a 30-year Pierpont Beach resident who stood on the promenade with his wife Santina watching the pier.

"It's such a shame," Santina Elton said.

City officials held an early afternoon news conference at the base of the pier, saying design and construction flaws have not been ruled out.

Public Works Director Ron Calkins said the city will hire an engineer who was not involved in the design of the structure to conduct an independent analysis.

"We think we're going to get some clues about how the damage occurred," Calkins said.

This much appears clear: The powerful 18-to 20-foot ocean swells came from the west, slipping past the Channel Islands,

Ventura County Star, December 14, 1995

Camarillo surfer lost in big swells

SEARCH: *16-year-old left his friends to catch some bigger waves at Faria Beach.*

From staff reports

The Coast Guard feared a 16-year-old surfer from Camarillo was lost at sea north of Ventura Tuesday night. The youth had failed to return to shore after telling his buddies he wanted to paddle farther out into the storm-swollen surf, authorities said.

Jaren Coler, who was described by officials as a surfer with "average skills," went surfing about 1 p.m. and was last seen at 5 p.m. when they were surfing at Faria Beach, about 7 miles north of Ventura.

Officials said the boy's surfboard had not been found, which they said could mean he was still floating on it. Coler, a junior at Camarillo High School, was wearing a thick red and black wetsuit that could combat the cold water for several hours.

"It's not too cold, so he should be OK for a while," said Petty Officer Edward Jackson of the Coast Guard station at Channel Islands Harbor.

Coler told his friends he wanted to paddle out a little farther to catch more of the 7-foot waves that have risen with the Pacific storm that moved into the county Tuesday. He was among scores of surfers lured out by the big waves, Jackson said.

"They went into shore and waited but he never showed up," Jackson said.

A 44-foot-Coast Guard boat was fighting rain, waves and limited visibility as they searched the water. The sheriff's department also had three units patrolling the beach.

A Coast Guard helicopter was going to join the search but was forced down due to low visibility, winds and rain, Jackson said.

Article dated December 13, 1995. Saved by Jaren's family.

Surfer Survives 10 Chilling Hours at Sea

By KENNETH R. WEISS
TIMES STAFF WRITER

VENTURA—Slipping off his surfboard, Jaren Coler awakened choking on seawater. His body erupted in spasms of coughing and then he vomited.

It was the third time he had thrown up. He was getting colder by the hour, starting to drift in and out of consciousness.

The shivering 16-year-old surfer from Camarillo recognized the signs of hypothermia.

"I didn't think I was going to die until I started to fall asleep," Jaren said Wednesday.

Sitting in the kitchen of his Camarillo home, the teenage surfer recounted how a quick after-school surf outing turned into a 10-hour ordeal during Tuesday night's storm—with Jaren bobbing helplessly beyond the breakers off Pitas Point north of Ventura.

He could see the flashlight beams of crews searching the rock-strewn shoreline of Faria Beach.

At first he couldn't paddle in, defeated by rip currents that swept him far out to sea. Later, he decided to wait, hoping the monstrous surf would calm so he could make a successful landing on the rocky shoreline.

But waves of fear began to wash over him when a Coast Guard boat disappeared. It had come within 200 feet on several passes and seemed to shine a spotlight on his face.

"I decided if I was going to die, I should die trying to get in.

Please see SURFER, B3

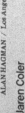

ALAN HAGMAN / *Los Angeles Times*

Jaren Coler

SURFER: Teenager Endures 10 Hours in Stormy Sea and Survives Ordeal

Continued from B1

rather than just stay out there," he said.

The Tuesday surf session began about 1:30 p.m. when Jaren and three friends from Camarillo High School drove up the coast on the promise of big waves—a welcome change to the flat surf in recent days.

The foursome slipped into the gated community of Faria Beach, using an access code to trigger the gate. After wriggling into their wetsuits, only Jaren and another friend, Jesse Kuhn, decided to paddle out into the breakers. One made a brief attempt at bodysurf, another stayed on shore.

The waves did not appear that big from the beach. Jaren said. But once in the water, Jaren and Jesse, soon faced fast 8- to 10-foot waves, each one breaking out farther than the next.

Jesse, a more experienced surfer, decided to call it quits and headed back to shore. Jaren plunged ahead, duck-diving under each advancing wall of whitewater with his 6-foot-1-inch board.

As soon as he made it past the breakers and caught his breath, he looked back at his friends on the shore.

"I started to paddle in and the current sucked me out," he said. "I felt like I was going back-ward."

The current soon swept him hundreds of yards out to sea. He waved helplessly to his buddies.

"It was getting darker and darker and we could hardly see him," said Chris Coker, 17, of Camarillo. Chris and Jesse called 911, the Coast Guard and Jaren's father.

Soon Jaren's parents and friends and neighbors convoyed on Faria Beach, joining county Sheriff's Department deputies and the sheriff's volunteer search and rescue team.

Faria Beach residents joined in the search. They turned on their deck lights to brighten the shoreline. They hung lanterns to Jaren's friends and dangled them and others in the search party with not success.

Jaren's father, Doug Coker, was worried sick. He climbed on the rocks to look for a sign of his only son, until sheriff's deputies persuaded him to wait inside their mobile command center, a re-vamped motor home.

"I was really worried he had a bad wave and hit his head on the board," Coker said. "As time went by, and I knew we had more experienced surfers out there. He's a strong kid."

The Coker family was particularly frustrated because the rain-snow made it too dangerous for a Coast Guard rescue helicopter from Long Beach to join in the search. And the weather kept a sheriff's helicopter grounded at the Camarillo Airport.

The Coast Guard's 44-foot boat and the search party on land concentrated on the coastline south of Faria. They judged that is the most likely place to find Jaren given the predominant side-shore current than runs down the coast.

But Jaren had been swept far-ther out to sea and was picked up by a countercurrent that took him

> "I didn't think I was going to die until I started to fall asleep. . . . I decided if I was going to die, I should die trying to get in, rather than just stay out there."
>
> JAREN COKER
> Surfer

up the coast.

"I started to hallucinate and imagine people. I was so hungry I could see hamburgers. I was so cold," said.

To take his mind off the cold, he thought about swimming to the Channel Islands, which he could see some nights surfing off Oxnard's Oxnard Beach and swim the waterfront to the Ventura County fairgrounds, where the lights from the county barn illuminated the waterfront.

But neither of these options had much of an appeal. On occasions had not challenge distractions. But without the daylight, best of surfers during the daylight hours.

"I was calm pretty much of the time," he said. Jaren tried to entertain himself by drawing designs in the ocean's surface.

The night had a red tide, causing the reddish algae that glow at night.

Each burst of water left a disorienting trail.

When a fish would go by, they would leave a blue trail," he said. "That kept me entertained."

Then there was a loud splash, and—then a fin break the water. He instinctively lifted his legs, to keep them from dangling in the water.

"When I saw the fin, it looked like a shark. My mind started playing tricks on me."

I turned out to be a dolphin. Two of the marine mammals came by at check him out, before swim-ming off into the darkness.

The birds were circling around me—he whole time I was out there, too." he said. Pelicans and sea gulls flew overhead, but they weren't friendly or had a they were tenacious intent.

"They were like vultures. I would yell at them, 'Get out of here,' they would fly off and then venture back slowly.

Jaren took heart when he saw the Coast Guard boat making sweeps, shining their spotlights into the dark sea. Five times, he

"I would fall asleep and fall off my board and wake up breathing water and get sick," he said. After getting sick three times, his aching and cooling left to discharge. He started shivering uncontrollably. And he sensed that time was running out.

So he decided to take his chances in the surf.

Jaren said he put his head down and begin to paddle as furiously as his rubbery arms would allow him. Each time, he could feel the wave was crashing down during a high tide, when the surf was at its peak.

The waves sneaked up behind him. He did not see it until it smacked on top of him, bashing his surfboard.

Jaren wrapped his arms around the board and held tight, he said. It seemed at last he was under a sense of direction. The next thing he knew, he had washed ashore on the rocky beach near where he entered the water.

He staggered up a set of concrete steps, cut into the sea wall with steps out into the sea wall with a shark breaking on his heels. Jaren slipped through the patio area of one of the homes, took several steps more and reached a gate as much as a pay phone outside the gated community.

Using a credit-card number committed to memory, he called home to ask his father and went to get Jaren back up and let him go. No big deal, he thought.

"Where's dad?" he asked his sisters. "Where are you?"

His sisters, in unison, screamed, in disbelief, "You're alive!" By Becky '14, had each picked up an extension.

He was capable of handling the phone at home during the 10-hour search, while his family was out searching for him, while parents and they said it was only a few hours and the morning," I said. No

He explained his location by the side of the road and lay down to

told of him, within 200 feet of him, with search lights reaching to his direction.

Waving a red and black wetsuit, Jaren knew he would not be easily spotted. So he tried treading water, holding his white surfboard over his head to catch their attention.

At the Coast Guard boat disappeared from sight, he grew truly scared. He was tired. He was growing colder. His arms were now sore.

ALAN HAGMAN / Los Angeles Times

Jaren Coker, 16, points to cracks in his surfboard. After 10 hours in a stormy sea Tuesday night, he reached shore tired but unharmed.

wait.

And promptly passed out.

Doug and Chert Coker were soon at Jaren's side, as were rescue workers and friends who helped with the search.

Neighbors Mark and Ruth Cousance brought Jaren a couple of ham and cheese sandwiches, which he promptly wolfed down.

Mark Custance, a former life-guard, had spent much of the night with rescue workers whom the chances of a happy ending had appeared slim.

On Wednesday, he recalled the words of one astonished searcher when Jaren had made it safely back to land.

"It never ends like this."

Jaren circa 2012, surfing off the coast of South America.

Acknowledgments

I am forever grateful for the many who have inspired and helped me along my journey of writing this book. Without their encouragement and cheering me along, my son's story would probably have remained unwritten.

Thank you to Bridget Cook-Burch, bestselling author and speaker, and Hannah Rose Lyon, editor and author, for lighting the fire deep inside and inspiring me to step out of my comfort zone and pursue this adventure.

Thank you to Michael D Young, author, singer and songwriter, for featuring the condensed version of this story in his compilation of miracles, entitled The Boss Level II.

Thank you to my amazing publishers and editors, Jayne Ann Osborne and Holly Boud Kolb of Merry Robin Publishing for approaching me and taking a bold chance on my work.

Thank you to my husband, Jack, who kept prodding me along to get this written.

Thank you to all the emergency search and rescue teams and the countless people who came that night to help search for my son, many of whom I will never have the privilege of personally thanking.

And to the many friends, neighbors and family members who came to our aid in the chaos of that night, I wish to thank you each from the bottom of my heart.

Thank you to the dear man, Bishop Thomas Martin. I will ever be grateful for his calm reassurance and love in the midst of such despair.

Last of all, my greatest gratitude to the God in Heaven, who is over all.

About the Author

Many years ago, when I felt more broken than whole, I penned the words: *Broken wings soar when courage takes flight.* This has become my personal motto and I have come to be a true believer in the power of overcoming obstacles that stand to crush or hinder me from becoming a better version of myself: an ongoing work in progress.

I was born in Southern Idaho, raised in Southern California and now reside in Northern Utah. I have lived in over forty homes, all without being in a military family. My life's journey is a reflection of the free spirited outlook I have on life. This free spirited outlook of mine has contributed to an entrepreneurial spirit from a very young age.

My 1st business venture was when at six years old, I would cut out comic strips and sell door to door, for a nickel each. From that time up until where I am now in my life, I have had many opportunities to spread my wings as a waitress, radio advertising sales person, hotel sales manager, corporate flight attendant, motivational speaker and real estate professional. Yet, my greatest accomplishment is my family, including being married to a wonderful man who happily puts up with me after all these years. Together, we have a combined family of six grown children and fifteen grandchildren.

I am a strong advocate taking on life's challenges, obstacles, and disappointments head on while turning them into advantages of personal growth, accomplishments, and success. I firmly believe every person has their own unique abilities, gifts, and talents to overcome any personal obstacles as they persist in achieving their own personal growth and successes.

***

If you enjoyed this book, please be sure to take a moment to review it on Amazon and/or Goodreads. Thank you!